The Baseball Gods

Before the Big Bang, the Bible and the Buddha there were...

The Baseball Gods

✦

A ball player's metaphysical guide to playing better baseball and living a better life

Ronald DiFabbio

iUniverse, Inc.
New York Lincoln Shanghai

The Baseball Gods
A ball player's metaphysical guide to playing better baseball and living a better life

iUniverse books may be ordered through booksellers or by contacting:

iUniverse
2021 Pine Lake Road, Suite 100
Lincoln, NE 68512
www.iuniverse.com
1-800-Authors (1-800-288-4677)

ISBN-13: 978-0-595-39732-7 (pbk)
ISBN-13: 978-0-595-84138-7 (ebk)
ISBN-10: 0-595-39732-8 (pbk)
ISBN-10: 0-595-84138-4 (ebk)

Printed in the United States of America

Dedicated to my Father

Who has ascended to the Pantheon of the Gods

Contents

Introduction

The title of this book is "*The Baseball Gods: A ballplayer's metaphysical guide to playing better baseball and living a better life*". Now, just the fact that you have the book in front of you means that you've probably been struck by the words, Gods, Metaphysics and Baseball, all in the same title and wanted to find out what this was all about. This is most likely the first time you've ever seen these three words put together in that way, and I would bet it's probably the first time it's happened in the history of western culture. With that said, you can be sure this is not your typical baseball instruction book, but I guarantee you it is indeed one. It is also a book that will help you to live a better life regardless of whether or not you are a baseball player. And the reason for this is because baseball, like everything else in this life, is just a symbolic reflection of the perfect energy that is existence. I know that sounds like a pretty lofty statement, but by the end of the book you'll wonder why you ever looked at life any other way.

Before I unleash the Baseball Gods on you, I need to define the words *Gods* and *Metaphysics* first. The only way to build a house is from the foundation up. And these two words are the foundation of an approach, which has bestowed on me a perspective that has produced better results on the field and peace of mind off it.

When I use the word *Gods*, I use it in reference to *energy*. The Gods represent the different forms of energy that affect us during our lives. This energy channels itself through our feelings, which then transforms itself into something material that we can see, touch and experience. It is our energy that has created the material reality we see around us on a daily basis. We create our own reality. And if you don't believe that's true or possible then take, for example, an inventor who creates a new material reality out of an *idea* or a *need*. Before the idea or need inspired him, the material entity didn't exist. But, after the inspiration, a new product is formed that can be touched and experienced by all. All of reality is formed in this way and if you really stop and think about it you'll see it can be no other way. We are the inventors of our own lives. So, if there is something in your life, in your game or about yourself that you don't like, just remember that you are responsible for it being there! You created it! And it is the *Baseball Gods* who generate all this energy to help us discover our true selves and invent our realities.

The word Metaphysics simply means the "Nature of Reality". And those who study it are looking to *define* what reality is. In western culture the question that has been pondered for centuries by the great minds is: Is reality Mind or is it Matter? (I left out Spiritual as an option because those who ponder these questions feel it is impossible to define religion with empirical proof. The Baseball Gods disagree with this assertion but not because they want to be a considered a religion, but instead because they represent spirituality in its purest form, inspiration and energy, which then becomes the empirical material reality we see around us.)

Well, after centuries of debate and life threatening run-ins with the entrenched dogmas of religion, the west, since the time of the "*Age of Reason*" has come down on the side of the material as its definition of reality. And it has been this lone, powerful conclusion that has shaped the world we've lived in ever since. Everything is defined materially in our culture, from our social status to how we love each other. It has been all encompassing. It is the reason we live in a material paradise. It is also the reason our culture lacks depth and meaning.

When we center the world on the material there is no room for meaning. Meaning becomes a commodity that we paste on to certain things to make it appear like our lives are important. But by doing this we kill the meaning in our lives without even knowing it. You see life cannot be meaningful when someone in your family dies and not when you are happy and playing Black Jack on the Vegas Strip. It either is meaningful all the time or it isn't. This is because *meaning is reality* and reality either is or it isn't.

This lack of meaning creates what the Existentialist call an "Existential Void" where feelings and the concept of something greater than ourselves is replaced by the material things we desire, which we know are transitory and do not last forever. And the problem is these material things will never provide what we really need, which is meaning. We've tried to fill that void with religion, but that hasn't worked either because even our religion has grounded itself in the material. Heaven is now a noun. It has become a person, place and thing just like all the other material creations we see around us. And the result has been disastrous. Never before has there been more violence, drug use and aberrant behavior than there is right now.

In the baseball world the material body is the center of the universe. How we learn to play the game as a child is based solely on the body's mechanics. Go to a Little League field some day and listen to the coaches. Everything they say is based on the mechanics of the body and the material reality. Even the pros primary focus is on their body whether they are trying to break out of slump or looking for that big hit in the clutch. And this, as you will see, is ass backwards.

When we learn to throw, hit and catch we are taught to focus on the mechanical aspects of these skills while never taking into account the person and his *feelings*. But if we truly examine the nature of reality we will see that we need to understand the *person first* before the material reality of the body! And though this may sound strange, the new metaphysics emerging from science, blended with the ancient metaphysics from Buddhism, Zen and the Tao, tells us that this is the way it should be.

You will see, as you read this book, that the material world we perceive around us is not the prime reality; it is instead the feelings or energy that the player brings to the game that *creates* his reality. For example, the western metaphysical way of correcting a hitter who is pulling his head off the ball on his swing is to give him physical/material solutions to the problem. A hitting coach will inform him to keep his head still and to keep his left side in. He may also move his feet or hands into a different position in order to achieve that end. But what is missing here and what has been missing in all of western metaphysics is that there is a *feeling* that is *making* the hitter yank his head off the ball. It can be anything from fear to anger to ego, but it is most definitely a feeling. And, until the hitter deals with that feeling, he will continue to pull off the ball no matter what physical prescription is given to him. It is this sole change in *perspective* that can change for the better how we play the game of baseball and how we live our lives....

Metaphysical Field of Dreams

No other sport has been treated so eloquently in history, literature and movies than baseball. It has created some of our culture's greatest heroes along with volumes of our most poetic and mythic verse. It has been a link to the innocence of youth and the endless summer days when it seemed like anything was possible. It has been an annual reminder of a time when our dreams were real and reality was as simple and pure as playing catch in our backyards with our fathers.

When I express my feelings about the game of baseball, I don't do so poetically (I'm not much of a poet) or creatively in fiction, although I can understand why people do. Baseball is a rich and beautiful game, which naturally lends itself to such pursuits. Instead, I see baseball philosophically as a meaningful experience and metaphysically as a means by which we can understand this meaningful experience.

Baseball has always been meaningful to me, although when I was younger it had little to do with philosophy or the nature of reality; it had to do with love. Baseball was the first love of my life. It was pure and uncorrupted like the love a child feels for his parents. That simple love was my reality and in retrospect it was the foundation for this book. But, as I grew older and life became more complicated, the innocence of youth, with its inexhaustible ability to dream, disappeared and was replaced with the awkward and sometimes destructive energies of adult life.

Of course, we all must grow up and maybe growing up and losing our innocence to the "real world" around us is part of the plan. Isn't that what the metaphor of Adam and Eve eating the Apple from the Tree of Knowledge was all about? Maybe this life we live is our education, our chance to understand what living means. And maybe what we're meant to learn is that there doesn't have to be a difference between the dreams of our youth and the stark realism of our everyday reality. Maybe heaven is here right now at this very moment. We just have to realize it....

The Path to the Gods

When I was four years old my father took a picture of me swinging a bat, which he placed in a photo album with the caption, "Our Future Major Leaguer". There was never a doubt in my mind or my heart what dream I was going to pursue or what my identity was going to be. I was going to be a baseball player and I was going to live out my father's dream of making the Major Leagues. And that wasn't going to be a bad thing because I loved my father and my mother and I wanted to make them happy more than anything else in the world.

As fate would have it, I was blessed with some of the tools necessary to become a big league ball player. I had exceptional eye/hand coordination and a power-house-pitching arm to go along with a competitive spirit second to none. In Little League I struck out nearly every batter I faced, and by the time I got to high school I was clocked at 90m.p.h. plus. My senior year I averaged thirteen strike-outs a game with just a fastball as my only weapon. An umpire told me that year he thought I was the hardest thrower in the state. (I lived in Connecticut.) Then as a junior in college I was ranked in the top ten nationally in Earned Run Average, in Division II, and had a phenomenal season that saw me beat some of the nation's top D-II and D-III teams. But, in spite of all the success I had in Little League and High School and was having in College, something inside me always felt troubled and in pain. I was rarely, if ever happy.

In Little League I was highly emotional and could never accept failure well with myself or anyone else. I would cry after I struck out and become angry at a teammate after he made an error. A common scene for me was throwing my glove in the air in disgust after witnessing a screw-up by one of my teammates. I was unforgiving in my relentless pursuit of perfection.

In High School and Babe Ruth baseball, I could throw the ball so hard it struck fear in the opponent, but I never had any idea where it was going. Every time I took the mound I never knew what to expect. Most of the time I felt like an alien in my own skin. I had no idea what my body was doing. It was as if I were detached and separated from it. Also, I was jealous of anyone else good and desperate to succeed as if my life depended on it.

Then in my senior year of college, after three successful but typically emotional years of college pitching, everything began to cave in on me and I began to falter badly, panic and completely lose control of my ability to pitch effectively. I felt so much pressure to succeed that I was coming apart internally. It even got to the point where one day I walked into the school infirmary and broke down in front of a nurse and wept while purging my feelings of inadequacy because I was blowing my chance of getting drafted into pro baseball. "If I don't make the pro's", I moaned, "I was nothing, no one."

What I didn't know then and wouldn't understand for another fifteen years was that there was a group beings working on me, prodding me and planting seeds inside my spirit that would one day take root and grow into a way of looking at life that would answer all of my questions and lay to rest the demons that had haunted me my whole life. Those beings were the *Baseball Gods* and this is the story of how I met them and how they changed my life…

It all started thirty years ago on a Little League field called "The Pit" in East Haven, Connecticut. The particular event happened during a typical Little League game complete with overzealous parents and eager kids, but it managed to wedge itself into my memory where it has remained as a seminal moment in my life to this day.

The play probably appeared rather mundane to any one of the rabid parents watching the game, and I'm sure if one were to interview any of the players or spectators afterward it would be doubtful that any of them would have remembered it at all. But, for me, it ended up being the seed that would grow into a major life-altering event thirty years down the road. What it did was to kick start me down a philosophical path that has, after many twists and turns, morphed into a way of looking at baseball and life…

I can remember the at-bat as if I were standing at the plate this very moment. It's strange how we sometimes can't remember something from two days prior, but something thirty years ago can be remembered in detail down to the sights, sounds, smells and feelings of what we were doing as if it had just happened. Actually, it's not strange at all because it's a measure of how *important* certain events are in our lives. It's the dynamic moments that stick out. The moments when, for one reason or another, we are pulled out of the tedious reality we often find ourselves in and are thrust into a moment of great depth and meaning. It is my contention that ones life should be chocked full of these moments, but most of the time that is not the case. Psychologist and Self-Actualization guru Abraham Maslow called these moments "peak experiences" and felt they were a key ingredient in the Self-Actualization or growth process. Thoreau also alluded to these moments or lack thereof as his inspiration for leaving the city of Boston to live in the woods surrounding Walden Pond.

I'm sure to the casual observer the at-bat was just another in a long line of innocuous Little League at-bats. But, from my perspective, every at-bat was a matter of life and death because my father was a perfectionist who would settle for nothing less than perfection from me. It was in this usual state of heightened expectations that I stepped into the batter's box and readied myself to hit.

I was a notorious first pitch hitter (for reasons I will discuss later) and on this occasion the pitcher threw a fastball on the outside part of the plate. I focused on the incoming pitch and stayed back like I was taught and drilled a base hit to right field. I could still feel the relief in my body as I watched the ball jet out to the right fielder. I had gotten a base hit and I had heard my father cheer in approval. I was safe until my next at-bat; at least that's what I thought. As I began to casually trot down to first base and shake the fear out of my body, I noticed something that sent a shot of electrically charged panic through my nervous system. The right fielder had fielded the ball cleanly, which was a rarity for a right fielder in Little League Baseball, and he was getting ready to throw the ball to first base to get me out!

Now, if you have ever played baseball then you know that getting thrown out at first on a base hit to right field is akin to "Original Sin". Trust me, when you have a father who expects perfection, there is no worse way to reduce a successful at-bat into an at-bat from hell than to get thrown out at first on a base hit to right. And, unfortunately, that was the horrific scene unfolding before my eyes.

I raced as fast as I could toward first base (unfortunately I was not born fleet of foot) and lunged at the bag with my long, lumbering legs stretched to their limit. As my foot slammed down on the base, the ball popped into the first baseman's glove at exactly the same time. (Another miracle that the right fielder threw a perfect strike to first base) I held my breath and waited for the umpire's call. Every fiber in my body braced for his decision. A split second later I heard the call. It was OUT!

Instantly, I began to fill up with a mixture of extreme embarrassment and rage. I was embarrassed because I knew deep down that I had dogged it down to first and got caught napping. Also, I was filled with rage at the umpire because I knew I'd never hear the end of it from my father.

I argued vehemently that a tie was supposed to go to the runner, but to the umpire's credit he just looked at me and said: "a tie doesn't go to the runner when the runner isn't hustling." Now, of course, at the time I didn't want to be taught a lesson from some umpire that I could care less about, especially when I knew I'd have some explaining to do when the game was over, but none the less he did succeed in planting that seed inside me. He probably thought he was just passing along a simple lesson about hustle to kid who would forget it two minutes later, but it was lesson that was never forgotten and one that eventually became one of the inspirations that led to the writing of this book.

As the years progressed and I played High School, American Legion, and College Baseball and then as a High School Baseball Coach, I saw the same lesson resurface over and over again in a variety of different ways, and that's when it began to really sink in. That simple play, years earlier, was much more than just a case of not hustling. It was a portal through which I could crawl and gain insight into the questions I've pondered all my life. Baseball it seemed was not just a game but also a *mirror* that reflected back to me who I really was and am.

Let's flash forward now twenty-five years. I'm the Pitching Coach of my old High School Baseball Team and I notice, as we're in our pre-game warm-ups for a league game we need to win, that my players have zero intensity or focus and are talking about everything else *but* baseball. I deduce that the reason for this is because the team we are playing is *awful* and hasn't won a league game in almost ten years. We should beat them handily and the kids know it. But this deduction only alarms me more and I begin to implore my players to get focused and to wake up because anything can happen in one game. "I've seen it happen many times before" I say. "And they're not that bad this year. They've already played a couple of close games. If you let a team like this hang around into the later innings they start *feeling* they *can* win. You have to bury them right from the start". But the response I got from the players was ho-hum. "Come on coach" they said, "this team sucks." At that point, I knew there was no chance of reaching them so I just shook my head and hoped for the best.

Well, we played the game and what happened was like something out of a bad dream. Everything that could go wrong did and we lost 5-4. Now, it's not like we made a ton of errors or pitched poorly. As a matter of fact, we didn't do anything physically poor that day. It's just that *everything* went against us. After the game, a parent said to me: "If we didn't have bad luck then we wouldn't have had any luck at all today". I just nodded, grunted and kept walking.

It was the most incredible thing I'd ever seen in thirty years of organized baseball. Every ball we hit was a laser, but right at someone. And every ball they hit was a dunk, a bleeder or a dying quail and they *all* found holes. Then, to top it off, every umpire's call went against us. It was like watching a Shakespearian Tragedy. We never had a chance.

After the game, the kids naturally blamed the umpires. They bitched and moaned about the lousy calls while I just listened. I also overheard the parents blame the umpires, but I didn't listen to their excuses. I knew exactly what had happened, but I wasn't sure if anyone else did. As we walked back to the locker room, I tried to broach the subject with our dejected Head Coach: "The Baseball Gods", I moaned, "That's what happens when you don't respect them. They come back to bite you."

He looked at me with a strange and quizzical look and said: "What do you mean the Baseball Gods?"

Now, at this point, I wasn't going to get into a spiritual/metaphysical discussion regarding the relationship between energy and results so I boiled it down. "Bad things happen when you don't have the right attitude" I said, and that seemed to suffice for him. He wholeheartedly agreed. "God damned kids were flat today. They took the game for granted and got burned. But Christ almighty we couldn't get a call to save our lives either. The umps were awful."

I wanted to say at that point: *"yeah but haven't you ever noticed that the bad breaks and lousy calls always go against the team that doesn't have the right attitude or is flat?"* But I didn't say that. I just decided to wrap our discussion with: "Yeah but luck comes to the well prepared" and I made my way into the locker to digest the whole miserable experience.

The frustrating thing about that game for me was the fact that it was and is virtually impossible for a coach to *put* the right attitudes, values and thoughts into a player's heart and mind. Those things have to be instilled in them by the player's parents long before he gets to me. There are things a coach can try, (and I will discuss some of these later) but ultimately for any change to happen it has to be understood that it is not baseball we are playing or coaching, it is life. It is the love that one *feels* for the *game* that is at issue here, not for oneself or ones individual performance. It is, in the end, about something much bigger than our selves. It is about the Gods...

In Greece, long before the birth of Christianity, the Greeks assigned Gods for the various natural phenomena they couldn't understand as well as Gods for every possible human experience one might go through. Besides the Gods that we are most familiar with like Zeus and Apollo there were Semi-Gods, Spirits, Titans and Monsters and all of them represented some aspect of human emotion and feeling whether it be passion, unrequited love, fear, anger or rage. You name it and the Greeks had a God for it.

All the Gods, Semi-Gods, Spirits, Titans and Monsters were also given some form and action with which they could be identified. They were adorned with certain symbols, like serpents, wings, thunderbolts or bows and arrows that represented whatever they were supposed to personify, and they all had a wonderfully rich story or myth that drove the lesson home. The Titan Atlas, for example, whose likeness graces the cover of this book, was given the responsibility of bearing the weight of the world on his shoulders as punishment taking up battle against Zeus.

The Gods and the Mythology created around them were explanations for things people couldn't understand much in the same way science now explains things to all of us that we don't understand. If you angered the Gods by not giving them their due respect or if you "broke their rules", then you could expect retribution. It was the Greeks symbolic way of saying that everything has its own energy and that energy is real and must be respected if you wanted good things to happen in your life. They didn't know scientifically that energy existed and that all life is made of energy, they just *felt it.*

When we view the Greek Gods now it is in a comic way. We imagine them bowling on Mount Olympus as an explanation for thunder and we arrogantly laugh because we know scientifically this is absurd. The clashing of hot and cold air masses makes thunder. But is the concept of Gods really that absurd? I don't think so. Many successful western cultures in history, like the Native Americans, Mayans, Celtics, Ancient Greeks, Egyptians and numerous lesser known Pagan cultures made a connection between the energy of man and his surroundings and it worked quite well for them. And some, like me, might argue it worked better than our science does for us today.

I think the greatest aspect of their perspective was the fact that there was *participation* built into their equation. But now, there is no such participation. We are separate from the workings of Science and God and ultimately from each other because we base reality on what is rational and measurable not on what we feel.

What we have replaced the Gods of our ancestors with is our monotheistic religion and the rationality of science. We have one Supreme God who is nameless, faceless and ultimately unknowable because it has no real connection to our *everyday lives,* and we have the stone cold rationality of science that we *feel nothing for* because it is based on pure reason.

In ancient times (pre monotheistic thought) there was no separation between God and the Material Reality they lived in. They were one in the same. When it thundered there was a symbolic *and* empirical connection. God and Science happened at the same moment and you *felt* it as the thunderclap pounded in your chest. You knew the thunder *meant something* in relation to your life. There was a *connection* and that is my point. The Greeks were not helpless beings under the control of some Supreme God they couldn't communicate with. They felt they were beings filled with many different kinds of energy from love, to fear, to anger, to jealousy, to apathy, to confidence, to enthusiasm (from the Greek word ethos) and that these energies interacted with the energies of the world around them and could be tapped into to change the course of their lives. So in effect they *were* in control of their lives. They were *responsible* for making things happen both positively and negatively and that *is something,* which is short supply in today's world.

There is a situation in baseball, which illustrates this perfectly. Let's say we have a pitcher in a tight spot. The bases are loaded late in a one run game and the count on the batter is three balls and two strikes. The pitcher in this case is *aware* of the batter's weaknesses *and feels* that a curve ball is the pitch to throw because the batter is a dead red fastball hitter. But the pitcher is *afraid* to throw the curveball because he doesn't have as much *confidence* with the curve as he does with the fastball. Also, he's afraid to walk in the tying run because he knows that walking in the tying run is an unforgivable offense in baseball. So what does he do? Does he give in to his fears and throw the fastball or does he face his fears and throw the curveball, which he *feels* and *knows* is the right pitch?

Well, let's say in this case the pitcher lets his fears get the best of him and he throws the fastball instead of the curve. He reaches back to throw but there is *doubt* in his spirit. There is the negative energy of fear *attached* to this pitch and that fear *will diminish* the effectiveness of that pitcher's chance of retiring the hitter. It will make him grip the ball tighter or do a hundred other different physical things associated with the energy of fear and doubt, which will then cause him to make a bad pitch that will either be a ball or get ripped for a hit.

Now, maybe the pitcher will be fortunate because the batter in question has confidence issues as well. Maybe he's been mired in a slump or has some personal problem that is sapping him of *his* positive energy, which then will result in his energy being even *lower* than the pitcher's and thus will make him fail. This result is possible, but don't count on it. And why leave it up to chance? Why not take *control* of your own fate? And anyway, in the long run, regardless of the outcome of the particular situation, ultimately the pitcher's fear and lack of trust in his skill *will* come back to haunt him somewhere down the line against a more confident hitter and probably when he needs it the most. It's all a battle of energies and that's what those Greeks and their Gods were trying to say. They weren't cartoon figures. They were to be taken as seriously as the image of Christ on the Cross-or a scientist performing an experiment…

There are many Gods in the game of baseball and each and every one of them can affect the outcome of the game. But the *Baseball Gods* have a greater significance than just the final score of a game. They are guides who show us who we really are. They are the reason we throw our helmet in disgust or destroy the water cooler. They are the answers to all our questions. Questions like: Why did that call go against me? Why do I get nervous in a big spot? Why did I swing at that bad pitch? Why can't I concentrate? Why am I rushing on the mound? Why am I lunging at the plate? Why am I trying to kill the ball? And ultimately and more importantly: Who am I? Because I guarantee you that if you don't know who you are it *will* show up on the field as all of the problems I just mentioned.

The Gods tell us everything we need to know about ourselves, both good and bad, and give us the opportunity, by forcing themselves into our awareness, to pin point the trouble spots and to change them. That is all they do. They prod and probe us in an effort to get us to learn and they do it by attaching themselves to the things we love most. In my case it was and still is baseball. In someone else's case it might be golf or basketball or tennis. And still in others it might be a boyfriend, a girlfriend or a spouse. It doesn't really matter what or who it is as long as it is grounded in love.

Now, before I get to the *Baseball Gods*, who are waiting patiently for me to introduce them, I want to first talk about something I've alluded to, but haven't identified yet, called *awareness*. It is the God's sole purpose for being. It is their mantra. They want us to have more awareness of ourselves, others and of something *greater* than ourselves called God, universal consciousness or whatever name you want to give it. The reason for this is because it is within the veiled walls of awareness that *reality* exists!

The best way to start off describing awareness is by trying to illustrate it with an example because any other form of explanation comes off sounding too mystical. Have you ever had a game or a moment in your life where everything just clicked and you could do no wrong? Like time was moving in *slow motion* and you could react at the exact moment you needed to? For example, you're at the plate and the pitcher throws you an off speed pitch and you're not at all taken by surprise and lunging at it foolishly. You are in perfect balance in neither an aggressive state nor a defensive state. You *act within* the situation exactly as it's happening and are in *union* with it hitting the ball on the button. And then, after the event happens, you have a picture of it in your memory that lasts for the rest of your life. Every sight, sound, smell, touch and feeling can be recalled instantaneously and the moment is relived as if it happened a few seconds ago. *That* is awareness.

Zen Buddhist's have been talking about awareness for centuries in relation to the Art of Archery and Flower Arrangement, but their philosophy can be drawn out to include any sport, craft or passion you may have. The Zen method for achieving awareness is simple in its scope yet challenging in its execution. What the Zen Archer or in our case the Zen Baseball player does is repeat the movements involved in his skill over and over, day after day and year after year until he puts his mind, his emotions and his desires to sleep and *becomes one* with the *feeling* of the movement. It is this single minded repetition that acts like a one point meditation and creates a state of nothingness that breaks down the ego and allows the participant to gain the perspective of one who now sees the forest instead of the trees. (I will talk about this more later when I cover the God of Repetition) There is no longer an Archer and his Bow and Arrow trying to hit a target, but an Archer, a Bow, an Arrow and the Target together at the same moment as *one.* Just as there is no longer a pitcher *trying* to hit a catcher's target, as if he were separate from it, but a pitcher who *is the target.* He doesn't *try* to hit it. He performs his act, from a perspective of devotion, until the ball is in the catcher's glove as if it were *always there.* As a consequence of his awareness there is a result. The arrow hits the bull's eye and the pitcher hits the catcher's mitt.

But, even though I talk of hitting a ball or a mitt or a target, there are no "tangible goals" that the *Baseball Gods* are concerned with. There is only the *process* and the *journey*, because we are all a work in progress. There is no goal in terms of a finished product, like coming in first or being given a trophy or money. The finished product is important only in that it is a symbolic result. You may very well win the game and achieve fame and fortune, but the actual result is the process and the elevation or evolution beyond the Mental (*ego gratification*) and Physical World (*fame and fortune*) and into the domain where pure energy exists. It is a place that is hard to describe in words. That's why spiritual texts always sound so vague when read aloud. It has to be *felt.*

(It should be noted here that by saying "winning isn't what matters" is not an *excuse* for losing. The Gods hate nothing more than a team or an individual who loses and then tries to absolve himself from learning any lessons by saying that "it's not whether you win or lose it's how you play the game". The Gods will punish you harshly for that attitude so I would be careful as players or coaches before you use that excuse. Take my word for it you won't get a break the rest of the season.)

The *Baseball Gods* represent energy and they want us to realize that hitting the inner target is what is important. The inner target or feelings are what create the material results we are hoping for, and only until we have hit that inner target can we ever really have any peace of mind and happiness with our results. This is why there are many who have achieved great feats and have basked in the glow of success, but in their everyday *lives* there is only a trickle of love and only fleeting moments peace. And yet there are many who have not achieved the highest level in their chosen field, but *have* achieved the absolute highest level they are *capable of* and thus have become *aware* and are at peace. They have *transcended themselves* into a state better than their ego or their culture can produce. They have reached Mount Olympus and they are immortal. That is why they say the best coaches are those who weren't the best players. They drew *everything* possible out their talent and they *loved* the game for the game's sake, not for what it could bring them, and thus they learned about themselves. It is analogous to the kid who grew up poor and had to *overcome* the odds to achieve, as opposed to the rich kid who was handed the finest of everything without *earning* it. Who would you rather have in a foxhole with you? Sure, both may end up successful, but one has character chiseled into his features while the other may or may not. In baseball terms it's like comparing the pitcher with the million-dollar arm and a five-cent head to the pitcher without as much talent who has had to use his head and his heart to succeed. Who would you want pitching an important game for you, or marrying your daughter, or watching your back, or as a close friend that you can count on? Now, I don't mean this a condemnation of money but instead the attitudes, intentions and *energy* it often times will create. Money and wealth is, like everything else, spiritual in its nature and meaningful, but it is our *attachment* (as the Buddhist's would say) to the material world and our belief that it is the core of reality that causes us to miss the symbolism and ultimately the lesson.

So remember, as you read this book, the objective is not just to get better in baseball, although you most certainly will improve dramatically; it's to get better as a person, which in turn will improve your baseball!

There are scores of other baseball books that preach many different methods for improving a player's swing or pitcher's motion. They'll tell you, if you're a hitter, to point your toes in a certain direction, keep your weight back, keep your left side in, roll your top hand over and oh yeah by the way, keep your eyes on the ball. Or, if you're a pitcher, they will have you holding your hands higher or lower—they'll shorten or lengthen your stride or they'll have you constantly searching for your perfect arm slot while all the time telling you to focus on the mitt. It's a wonder players perform well at all with the information overload going on in their heads. But what many coaches fail to do is to *understand the person*. And that's where all the answers reside!

When I teach baseball, I spend as little time as possible teaching mechanics as a remedy for problems. Instead, I try to enlighten the player to the *values* (energy) that might be inhibiting the individual's natural and unique ability to perform the act. For example if you are yanking your head off the ball because you're trying to kill it, then find out *why* you're trying to kill the ball. There is a *feeling or value* that you are *transferring* to the *act* of trying to hit the ball, which is causing you to try and kill it. What you need to do is to fix *that!* Once you remove the reason then the body takes care of itself and does what it knows how to do. Your body doesn't want to try and kill the ball; it's your values, feelings and ultimately your *energy* that is driving the action. It is, as you will soon find out, the Gods...

Up until now I have talked about the *Baseball Gods* mostly in terms of concepts, philosophies and ideas, but as I introduce you to them and bring them into the concrete everyday world you'll wonder, just like I did, how you managed to miss them all along. I liken it to one of those images that you stare at until it becomes a picture of some scene. On the surface it looks like a bunch of innocuous patterns, but within those patterns is a whole other world. It's all in the perception and it's about time we stare at the image of western culture and see beyond the veneer of its material nature and into its true reality, which is that of pure energy. The proof is out there just waiting to be integrated into our consciousness and the Gods are out there as well doing their best to wake us up from our slumber...

So, who are these gods? What are their names? How do I recognize them? And lastly, how do I communicate with them? I have referred to them as just energy, but they really are much more specific than that. Like everything else, they start out as energy, but then they *become* tangible. They are separately pieces of a puzzle that when finally put together make us whole. They are like hundreds of fire flies that when taken individually give off just a speck of light but when brought together can illuminate the portions of our world that have been longing to see the light of day. And that is what they help us do. They guide us, torch in hand, as we stumble along in the darkness of this thing we call life. They help us to see that we are not victims of fate but masters of our own domain...

So, here we go. It's time to step up to the plate, take our practice swings, adjust our batting gloves, knock the dirt from our spikes and ready ourselves for a trip into the domain of the Gods. They are a demanding group and they don't miss a thing. When Jason and his Argonauts went in pursuit of the Golden Fleece he encountered numerous obstacles set up by the Gods and all of them tested his will and his character and the Baseball Gods are no different. They exist to shape our character. They chisel away who we think we are until we discover who we *really* are!

The Major Gods

Since meeting the Baseball Gods some eight years ago, I have gone into every season thinking I've come to face with every possible situation a God can throw at me, and that all I needed do was some fine-tuning and that would be it. But, of course, that thinking was and is naïve because with every new season comes new lessons and discoveries that challenge everything I think I know about myself. The learning never stops and the growth, which is often times painful, never ends. And now, as I ready myself for the new season, I've finally realized that it will be no different. There will be no fine-tuning and no free lunches. Everyday, whether the lesson turns out to be painful or joyous, will be a day filled with study, introspection and reflection. That is the way the Gods want it.

You see at forty-two I still play competitive baseball in the M.S.B.L. (Men's Senior Baseball League) in Hartford, Connecticut. It's a league for old geezers like myself who still want to feel the anticipation of spring and the start of a new baseball season. It's the same feeling I had when I was eight years old and couldn't wait for my first little league game. That's why I still play baseball in middle age. It's because it makes me feel like I'm a kid again, reborn after a long hard winter where the everyday realities of life weigh heavily on my shoulders. But with every passing season, it still amazes me how much younger I grow in my heart. And by season's end, another chapter has been written in what sometimes seems like a never-ending book...

THE GOD OF EGO

I'm going to lead off my discussion of the Gods by looking at their main guy, the God that makes everybody else go, their M.V.P. candidate. This God is all-powerful and must be recognized and given its due respect because if you don't then all the other Gods won't have a chance to see the light of day, and you will languish in the land of ignorance forever. It doesn't matter if you are a great player or not because this God doesn't care about your ability; it just wants to see if it can get you under its spell. And, if you *happen to be* a great player you will rarely if ever find contentment and wisdom in your accomplishments. Likewise, if you're *not* a great player it will be doubtful that you'll ever improve.

The God I'm talking about is the God of Ego. It is bright, brilliant and tremendously seductive. It will weave its way into your subconscious and completely take over your life if you let it. It will help you to paint such a glorious picture of yourself that you will be powerless to do anything else but stare at it. It will wrap its tentacles around you and hold you in a vice grip from which few have ever escaped...

As with every God you will be introduced to in this book, there are two different and distinct perspectives from which you can worship. You can either travel down the path that says life has meaning or you can choose the path that says life is nothing more than a random series of meaningless events that we give meaning to. As I discussed earlier, there are no other choices. Every single thing that encompasses life on Earth, whether it is material or non-material in nature, can fall into either of these two categories neatly and without exception.

If you choose to look at life as meaningful, you will keep this God in check and assimilate its energy into your life until you become one with it. Then you will be on your way to knowing who you are. And your pilgrimage to the pantheon of the Gods will be underway.

On the contrary, if you choose to see life as not meaningful, but as a *means* to satisfy your earthly wants and desires, then the God of Ego will blind you from seeing all the other Gods and you will be forever at their mercy, troubled and lacking the inner peace and contentment that comes from being in touch with your true feelings. When you are alone you will cower at the feet of the God of Fear. When you lack faith, which is all the time, you will be at the mercy of the God of Anger. You will be so tired of trying to out run your past and so desperate to control your future that you will miss the moment you are living in entirely. Your soul will be a cup that can never be filled. Your world will suffer from a thirst that will never be quenched because, without meaning, your life will become vacant and soulless. And you will be powerless to do anything about it…

The enigmatic world of the God of Ego has two distinct and powerful sides, one that illuminates and one that dominates. It is quite simply the most powerful force that exists on Earth today. It can transform your life or it can lure you into a journey of wants and desires that will eventually end with the loss of your soul.

The development of the Ego *is* natural and essential for the healthy development of a child, but it must be handled carefully or it will turn into an uncontrollable force. An analogy would be Nuclear Energy. It is a clean and efficient source of energy if controlled and in the right hands, but if used with the wrong intention it is a force capable of mass destruction. Such is the case of the Ego.

You've all heard the terms Freud used to describe the stages of psychological development in a person. They are the Id, Ego and Super Ego. The Id is concerned with the primary and primitive needs or drives of a person. The Ego is the "self" or what one "feels about ones self" that is unique and distinct from all others and the Super Ego is the ability to incorporate the morals and values of a society into one's life. All these stages are important and each one has to be balanced and stable if the others are to develop normally. No single one should be allowed to dominate the other because when this happens trouble is just around the corner.

If we look at the stages of development we see that each must be met if we are to have healthy individuals and a healthy society. The Id is associated with the security that comes from having a roof over our head, food to eat, the physical and emotional comfort of our parent's touch, and most importantly the boundaries we learn in order to protect ourselves from harm both physically and emotionally. If the needs of the Id have been met, the Ego will develop naturally giving us a sense of who we are, what we think and how we *feel*. We will be "comfortable in our own skin". And lastly, once we have our basic needs met and have a sense of who we are then we can progress to our Super Ego and find our place in the world. But if along the way one of the components of the Id or Ego are neglected or abused we run into trouble and we have "issues", which can hinder us in our attempt to integrate into the culture around us…

The Baseball player who pays homage the God of Ego cares only about himself. He has shunned his feelings in favor of the material world. He has decided to define himself by what he acquires materially instead of who he is spiritually. The world revolves around him. He worries about his statistics first and helping the team win second. He doesn't do the little things on or off the field like *Sacrificing* (literally and figuratively), *building relationships*, showing *feelings* and *caring* about his teammates. He doesn't care about these *healthy* Gods. He only cares about one God, *himself.* He is a disciple of the dark side. He is Darth Vader in a baseball uniform and he can tear apart team unity by his selfishness. He doesn't trust others and is *never* vulnerable. Few know what he is thinking and fewer ever will. *Nothing is ever his fault.* He has no patience for other people's mistakes and blames his own on everyone else. And most of all, he doesn't *love the game.* The game is a means by which he can *glorify* himself. For him life has lost meaning. He has given up on love and has forgotten that he is just one part of the puzzle of life that he *shares* with every other soul on the planet, not separate, but as one…

Spotting an egotistical ball player is usually an easy job for a coach, but fixing it may be another thing all together. The reason for this is because the chances are, if the child is egotistical, then probably one or both of the parents are egotistical as well. The apple never falls far from the tree. And so, the coach or the teacher is in a 0-2 count right from the beginning. But there is hope. There is always hope…

How do we help an adult or a child see that the God of Ego is ruling his life? It's a question that presents us with a paradox. We need to help the person see that the world doesn't revolve around him, but the problem is he thinks this way because he's incapable of seeing things that don't fit his image of himself. It's like trying to tell an alcoholic that he's an alcoholic while he's drunk. It's impossible. And in the case of our player, he's drunk on the image he has of himself as a baseball player or whatever it is that's floating his boat…. So, the question is: what do we do?

Well, the first thing you do in the case of the alcoholic is to remove the alcohol from the equation. And in the case of our egotistical player, you remove that which is making him drunk, namely the baseball. (Although, it should be noted that his Egoism goes much deeper than the game of baseball. Baseball may be just one of many areas where his Egoism has chosen to surface. But, in the case of our player, baseball is where we can confront it.)

The player's over inflated Ego *needs* to be fed and if the food he has chosen to satiate his Ego with is baseball then there is leverage from which to teach. It's a delicate job, but it can be done. Basically what you are doing, as a coach, is something the parent failed to do and that is to teach the child that, although we all must embrace our own unique, individual qualities, other people matter and must be respected. He needs to see that the team or the whole matters more than the individual. And lastly, he needs to reconnect with his feelings as the prime reality and realize that, to the Gods, learning is more important than statistics.

The ego-centered player is infected with a self-absorbed energy that must be changed and there are a couple of different angles I use to try and achieve that change. The first approach is biological in nature and uses the body to expose the true nature of the player to himself, which in turn forces him to question if he *really wants* to play baseball. The second is by redefining the meaning of love as a means of exposing the player's deluded image of himself, which then forces him to face the truth about who he really is. It, in effect, throws a mirror up in front of him that he can't help but see. This can be accomplished by injecting new ideas (energy) into the player's consciousness, which form boundaries (Id) that he must play within if he is to play at all…

The biological approach is by far the easiest to administer and is an effective short-term answer, but it does come with a warning. It may cause the player in question to quit without helping him to break the spell cast on him by his Ego. But, if that is the case, you'll have to take solace in knowing that he wasn't *ready* to face the truth about himself anyway. And that's okay because that's his right.

What I like to do at my practices is to work my players hard. I make them run and run and run. We do long distance running and sprints around the bases. We do 220's and 440's and Indian Runs. We practice stealing until they can hardly pick up their legs and exercises with their bats that leave their arms weary. The reason I make them do these exercises is not because I want to torture them, but because I want to introduce them to reality of hard work, which is a sure fire way to deflate their overblown Egos.

The reality of playing a sport is that you have to be physically fit. The connection between being physically fit and performing to one's maximum potential is obvious. But aside from the need to be physically better than an opponent, the process of working a body hard also helps to sharpen the mind's ability to focus, while at the same time helping to prop up a player's confidence if it is sagging. Knowing that you've worked harder than the man you are competing against is a great way to enter a contest.

The regime I put my players through forces them to reexamine if they really want to get their Ego high from playing the sport of baseball. It also gives them what might be their first glimpse into their character and their motives. This obviously won't result in a full transformation right away, but it plants the seeds. From that point, if the player hangs in there and I have him for three or four years he must adjust himself away from his selfish motives and over to the concept of team. He won't survive if he doesn't. I have seen many a player try to fake it, but eventually the player's *real* character comes to the fore and he either quits the team or commits such an egregious offense that he is dismissed.

I have had players go both ways. Some turn the corner and start their journey down the road of self-awareness while others have walked away in anger and moved further away from self-awareness. But, more importantly, both have had *experiences* and those experiences either good or bad will add up as they proceed in life until they hopefully lead to a healthy sense of self.

The second approach I use to help a player disengage from his overblown ego is to redefine the meaning of love for him. There has been a vast misconception that has penetrated our consciousness over the past twenty years and that is that love must always be *unconditional.* This phenomenon has been spreading across our culture like a bad cold and seems to have been passed down by a generation of parents who grew up, like me, in an environment that was overly strict, critical and extremely judgmental. They didn't like the way it felt and so they've done the opposite with their own children. The result has been a disaster equal in proportion to the mistakes of the past. Currently, we see a society so politically correct it is nearly paralyzed.

It is the parents who create in their children a deluded self-image by *never* being critical of them. If a child is clearly not very good and strikes out three times in a game and can't catch the ball, his parents won't say that he needs to practice more. They'll say: "don't worry son you played well" and only emphasize the positives thus giving the impression to the child that he *doesn't need to improve.* The child consequently grows up thinking that *everything* he does is good. His Ego is now overblown. And so, when the this child gets to me in high school and I inform him that his good is not good enough to be a starter or maybe even to make the team, the kid indignantly can't accept it. "How can that be?" He demands. "I've always been good because my parents have been telling me so my whole life." And that's when all hell breaks loose and irate parents vilify coaches because they can't accept the reality that their child may not be good at something. It harkens them back to their own feelings of low self worth that they don't want to face.

You see this person is not just an egotistical ball player; he simply doesn't have any sense of reality. In some ways, this can be more dangerous in the long run because this person doesn't have the tools to fight through the challenges of real life. He usually quits and retreats back into the protection of his parents and then as an adult spends his life medicating himself in some way to escape the void he feels inside. Look at the precipitous rise in drug use by teenagers and adults. They can't face reality and need to continue to find ways to escape it.

Life is hard work. It was never meant to be anything other than that. This doesn't mean it can't be enjoyable hard work, but it must be, at its core, hard work. If you want to keep your body in shape you must work it out. If you want to become more educated you must study hard. And if you want to understand the meaning of your life you must do the most difficult thing of all; you must face yourself. Love is not unconditional, nor was it ever meant to be. It is something, which must be earned with mutual respect, dedication and selfless motives...

Up until now, I have been talking about the Ego from a coach's perspective. I haven't yet talked about it from the perspective of the egotistical player who may be reading this book and there's a reason for this; it's because the egotistical player doesn't think there's anything wrong with him! His Ego won't allow it! He doesn't search for answers. He has all the answers already! So therefore he will, most likely, not be interested in this book...Or if he is reading this book his ego won't allow him to see himself as egotistical. He'll see it in others and point his judgmental finger, but he will never point that finger in his own direction.

We all know Egotistical people of varying degrees and we must deal with them everyday. We work with them, have romantic relationships with them and play baseball with them. They are everywhere because it must be said that being egotistical fits in nicely with the materialism of western culture. They thrive in our culture. Egoism is materialism/capitalism. They are one in the same. And that is why the west, though rich, is also so violent, spiritually bankrupt and cannot consume enough to fill the emptiness inside.

So the question remains: How do I delicately broach the subject of Egoism to any Ego Centered ball player or person who might be reading this book? I guess the best way to do it is to just describe some of the extreme qualities that an Ego Centered ball player might have and if that fits you well then...you can decide for yourself if it's something you might want to think about deeper or dismiss entirely.

If you have some of these qualities, but not all the time or not to the extreme, then you can look at the times when you do exhibit Egotistical behavior and learn from those particular moments because those are the ones the Gods *want* you to learn from! Very few humans fall into every extreme category, but it is easier for me to illustrate it for you with obvious examples. I mentioned some of these qualities earlier and now I'll cover a few more...

The Egocentric player looks down on and has no patience for those he feels are inferior to him, which is just about everyone. He doesn't *care* about his teammates. There is no *warmth* or genuine feeling. There is an aloof quality that separates him from what he considers the rabble. He isn't there to help out a teammate emotionally if he's struggling with a personal problem. People with personal problems are weak to him. He will never do the little things that help a team win unless he can achieve some degree of personal glory for the act. He trusts no one because he sees the worst in people. He puts himself first. He must always be in control of himself and those he chooses to have around him. He thinks he's the authority on everything and can never admit he's wrong...

What the Egocentric player doesn't know is that he is this way because he is the *opposite* of all that I have mentioned and it is these internal contradictions that block him from ever being truly happy. His happiness is built on quicksand that can disappear at any moment. His bravado is just a front to hide the uncertainty, confusion and loneliness that lay just below the surface.

There are questions you can ask yourself if you're still not sure if you are an Ego driven ball player. Look at your life and ask yourself, as honestly as you can, if it is filled with happiness, joy, self-reflection and selfless giving? (Forget about your batting average or how fast your fastball was clocked; they don't mean anything in the long run. The energy of life that binds us all together cares about them only in that they were given to you so you could learn. It cares about that which is eternal, not transitory.) Are people filled with happiness and joy when they are with you? Is there openness and caring given by you and received by you from others? Is there sacrifice and giving? Are you learning something new about yourself everyday and facing your fears? Do you understand that you are not the center of the universe? Are you *humble* before the game of Baseball? Because only by being humble will there be a chance at peace of mind.

Now, don't get me wrong, if you are an Ego driven ball player you will get your stats. You will win games. And if you have enough natural physical talent you will become a famous Major Leaguer. But the key is: will you be happy enough to be able to *enjoy it* and wise enough to understand what it means?

I have a perfect example to illustrate the Ego-centered ball player for you. My men's baseball league team was playing in a game recently and we were down by two runs going into the last inning. Our leadoff batter that inning was ahead in the count three balls and no strikes. Now obviously, at this point, everyone knew that he should take a strike because we needed base runners, but what did he do? He swung at the 3-0 pitch and flew out to left. When he came back into the dugout we asked him what he was doing swinging 3-0 when we were behind and needed base runners and his response was: "I'm too good a hitter to take a pitch right down the middle. That was *my* pitch and *I* don't take pitches like that". It wasn't about the team; it was about *him*. A wave of negativity swept through the bench and we went on to lose the game. The egotistical ball player doesn't realize what a negative impact his selfishness can have on his teammates. It can ruin teams. It doesn't have to be something overt; it's sometimes just the little, subtle things that add up to losses instead of wins.

As a side note here, I'd like to say that we pointed out this Ego problem to our teammate, but it had no impact. He didn't have an epiphany and the hard truth is he may never get one; although I hope for his sake he does. (But the truth is that the people we care about may never reach the high ground that we can see for them. And so it's up to us to deal with it in the healthiest way possible.) If he were someday to see the light he would see that despite all his talent and individual success on and off the field, his selfishness has taken its toll on his personal life as well as his baseball life. The two, as I've tried to show, will always go hand in hand...

And what about me? Am I an Egotistical player? Now, I know what you're thinking. If I were an Ego Centered player I wouldn't be able to answer the question honestly because my Ego wouldn't let me! But let me assure you that I am not an Ego Centered player with an *inflated* Ego. I'm the opposite side of the coin. I am a Low Self Esteem player with a *shattered* Ego.

As a child, all I was interested in was pleasing other people, namely my parents, as a way to try to feel good about myself. That's all I ever really wanted, to feel love because love was what I wasn't feeling inside. Nothing else mattered. Everything I did I did so I could gain their love. I had no self-esteem and no self-worth and that is not a healthy way to live. I gave more than I had because I was desperate to get something, anything in return. I viewed baseball as a vehicle to feel good about myself. Not because I thought I was *better* than everyone else like an Ego-Centered person would, but because I thought I was *worse* than everyone else. I gave everything I had to the game in an attempt to have some type of identity and purpose, but in the end I crumbled under the weight. Because remember, baseball cannot played in a healthy way if one is using it for self-serving purposes. *Baseball does not serve us; we serve it.* And that leads me to the next god, a god that I know more intimately than any other...the God of Self Esteem.

THE GOD OF SELF ESTEEM

The God of Self Esteem is closely related to the almighty God of Ego. The reason for this is because the Ego-Centered player and the Low Self Esteem player both have Low Self Esteem. But there is a major difference. The Egocentric player with Low Self-Esteem has found his answer in the world of self-glorification. He puts himself on the peak of the mountain because he can't survive anywhere else. He *needs* to be able to look down on others. Whereas the Low Self Esteem Player is in the valley hoping he can get something to grow. He only wants to feel love for who he is and to be loved by those around him...

So, what exactly is Self Esteem and how does it get low? Self Esteem is what people feel when they are in touch with their true feelings, which then makes it possible to know themselves and to find their place in the culture. It is these feelings or energy developed during our formative years that become the material reality of our "life" within the culture.

On the surface it all sounds quite simple and easy. All a parent has to do is to meet the specific needs (because no two children are the same) of the child and to nurture his or her feelings. From there the child will grow into an adult that is in touch with what it is feeling. But from the state of the world it is obvious that this is not as easy as it seems in theory. The reason for this is because our parents and our culture are not perfect and will never be, within the current framework of reality that we have in place. As long as the material world is recognized as the prime reality then we will always be in the dark searching for who we really are. The material reality will always come up short and leave us with an emptiness inside that our culture cannot fill. It is only when meaning and feelings replace substance as the prime reality that the emptiness disappears....

The Low Self Esteem ball player doesn't have an Ego. His Ego has been obliterated and he doesn't have the need to replace it with an inflated image of himself or material things like the Egotistical player does. He has no sense of self and no defined image of who he is. He doesn't feel worthy of love. He is constantly looking externally for a way to define his being because what's inside is ugly and misshapen. He feels that if he does something well, like a hit a homerun, then he is a good person. His entire self worth is overly conditional (the opposite of the overly unconditional self worth that Ego player feels) and ultimately unsustainable because it is based solely on "positive" results, which are an impossible standard to live up to.

The God of Low Self Esteem is birthed from the same womb as all the Gods and that is from the subconscious of the child as it *feels* and *absorbs* the world around him. It's these feelings that drive us when we grow older. As we grow from the innocence of youth, the mind, with its ability to think and reason materially, tries to sort through these feelings, but it's not equipped for the job and thus we spend our lives never really getting to the core of who we are or what this life is all about.

The mind/brain has absolutely no idea what do with someone who looks in the mirror and hates what he or she sees. It's great for running the systems of the body and interpreting the material stimuli from the world around us, but when it comes to understanding energy, euphemistically known as "the heart" it is clueless. That's because the heart is in the domain of the Gods and the God's care about our feelings not about the mind.

The Gods want us to *feel* that life means something and the method they employ to get us there is to take what we care about in life, like baseball, and use it *symbolically* to drive us away from the mind/material world and into the heart. The Gods know that once we start to do this our lives splits wide open like a watermelon revealing the answers to all the questions our hearts have felt and our minds couldn't answer.

When I cracked open my watermelon I noticed that when I played well and pitched a great game I felt better about myself. I felt like a good person. I would get compliments about my pitching and be happy that people liked me. And that was *not* good. Oh sure, we all like to do well and it's nice to have people say good things about us, but when we *depend* on it, well, that's when the tail starts wagging the dog.

I have battled this Low Self Esteem affliction my whole life like a drug addict battles his addiction. Only now that I'm in my early forties have I begun to see that I don't need to pitch well or hit well to feel good about myself. I know now that it's the *learning* that's important. It's the Gods that matter. If I pitch a great game and then don't look for the meaning, I am dooming myself to fail somewhere down the road. This is because the Gods want to be heard and it seems only in failure do we humans listen. We only pay attention when they are beating our brains out. But now, good result or bad, I look to see what my performances are trying to tell me about my life and *that's* how I judge whether or not I'm a worthy person. It has been that change in perspective that has made all the difference and has pulled me up from the bottomless pit of Low Self Esteem and into the light of Self-Worth. (It should be noted here that this perspective is not the one 99% of the people in western culture have. In the west it is about results and material things as proof of your importance and respectability. But the Gods…they only care about your heart. And in the end when the Gods come calling…only the heart can hear the call….)

Two years ago I represented Connecticut in an MSBL Regional Tournament for players thirty-eight years and older, in Albany, New York. We played well, like the multi-championship team we were, and made it to the final where I was chosen to pitch. I was nervous as always because the status of my self-esteem was on the line, but on the other hand I also loved pitching the big games because it gave me the opportunity to boost my self-esteem. It was and always has been a double-edged sword because a loss would end up validating what I've always feared about myself, that I wasn't a good player or person, and a win would give me the shot of self esteem I needed to keep me going. As it turned out, I ended up pitching one of the best games of my life and we won 4-0. It was a great game and it capped off a great year where I went 8-2 and had a 0.61 earned run average.

After the game, I said to my friend and teammate that I thought I might pack it in and put my forty plus body out to pasture. My rationale for giving up the game I loved was I figured "how could I ever have a better year?" I wanted to go out on top so I could feel good about myself. Of course, what I was forgetting was that I love to play the game. My Low Self-Esteem was so desperate for an outstanding final memory to hang my retired hat on that I was willing to give up doing something that I love to do!

Well, the new season came around and everybody wanted me to play. So, of course, I played, but I was scared to death that I would never be able to top the year I had prior and so…you guessed it…I didn't even come close. I had a lousy year in terms of statistics because my energy was full of Fear and Low Self-Esteem. I was so afraid I'd lose what little self-worth I had gained from the year before that I had *caused* bad things to happen. I ended up the year 8-8 and had some of my worst efforts in years. But you know what? It also ended being the best year of my life because I really started to see myself clearly. I had always been great at seeing how the Gods affected others, but now I was only focusing on what they were trying to tell me. And what they were trying to say was that I wasn't going to eradicate my Low Self Esteem by simply pitching well. I was going to change only when I began to change my perspective on life from one of material to one of meaning. But, in order to do that, I had to face yet another Major God that had been tormenting me whole life…The God of Fear…

THE GOD OF FEAR

If the God of Ego is the clean-up hitter and MVP of the Gods, then the God of Fear is most definitely their starting pitcher and Cy Young Award candidate. The God of Fear is pervasive and has its claws dug deeply into the heart and soul of every ball player and person who walks the earth. It is how we deal with this fear that determines whether or not we will reside in eternity with the Gods or languish on earth and suffer the slings and arrows of our misfortune.

If there were ever someone to talk about the God of Fear from an up close and personal vantage point, it would be me. Because of my low self-esteem I have always been a particularly vulnerable target for fear. I have always *needed* success to feel good about myself and this has made for a fertile breeding ground in which fear can flourish. But, as with all of the Gods I will cover, once you become aware of them and deal with them you can fight them off and in some cases use them to your advantage! There is an old saying: "what doesn't kill me makes strong" and this saying never applied more than when facing the mighty God of Fear.

Fear is a master at zeroing in on every weakness you might have and exposing it. It loves to do that. It thrives on finding those painful areas of the psyche and poking at them until you take notice. If you have any self-esteem issues, doubts about your talent, defects in your personality or issues from your childhood then you can be certain these will be fully exposed on and off the field by the God of Fear.

When I was younger I was so afraid to strike out, because of the obvious self-esteem draining implications, I used to swing early in the count just so I didn't have to face a two strike pitch. Even if it wasn't the best pitch to drive, I would swing at it anyway because I feared striking out so much. And, to make matters worse, I had such good eye hand coordination that I always hit the ball before I got two strikes on me. In turn, I didn't strike out much, but neither did I take full advantage of my potential as a hitter because a large part of being a really good hitter is being able to be selective and to hit a hitter's pitch instead of a pitcher's pitch.

The God of Fear is usually seen prominently displaying its talents during Little League baseball games. It is as if every action on the field is dominated by the fear of failure. The kids' *and parents'* emotions rise and fall as they succeed and fail throughout the game. Watch a little leaguer trying to catch a pop-up sometime and you'll see what I mean. It's as if the safety of the free world rests on whether or not the catch is made. His body is tense and contorted. His face is frozen in fear and there is a collective silence in the crowd until the ball either lands in his glove, on the ground, or bounces off his head, all of which produces a spasm of groans or cheers from the parents. But that being said, fear is an integral part of the maturation process because it sorts out the players who are there just because their parents want them to be, from the ones who truly want to play the game.

Fear is truth, albeit hard truth. It is an invaluable resource for finding out of what we are made. But like most truths, the lessons doled out by the God of Fear are painful to accept. The reason for this is because we rarely see ourselves for who we really are.

When coaching or playing the game of baseball it is imperative that fear is faced and dealt with because if it is an amazing thing happens. Fear loses all of its power and is replaced by another god, the God of Confidence. What happens when fear is faced is that you come out of the encounter and realize that it wasn't as bad as you thought it was going to be. The reason for this is because you've shined a light on the mysterious cloaked stranger and by doing so have taken away his greatest strength, which is his stealth and his connection to the deepest and most feared energy in the collective unconscious, the Gods of Death and Change. But I'm getting ahead of myself. For now, let's just see how the God of Fear fits into the game of baseball.

I'd like to go back to the example I gave you earlier when I explained how, as a little leaguer, I would swing early in the count because I was *afraid* of striking out. What I was doing then was giving in to fear. My self-esteem couldn't handle failure so I tried my best to keep a few feet ahead of it. But you can never out run fear. Oh sure you can try and there are those who run marathons daily, but fear is tireless in its pursuit and will win out in the end. It will get you eventually and in the process it will eat you up inside until you are a shell of your former self. Take a look around at people sometime and you'll see the fear on their faces as they do anything they can, from drugs, to sex, to gambling, to fame, to job security, to loveless relationships in order to keep their secret hidden. But there is only one-way to defeat fear and that is to face it head on and more importantly to understand what it *means*.

If we look at my experience as a little leaguer we can ask the question: What would have happened if, instead of swinging early, I accepted the fact that I was afraid and maybe took a strike or two? And the answer is…I might have struck out or I might have *gotten a hit!* But either way something more important would have happened. I would have *learned* something about myself and then maybe I would have come up with a *solution* to the problem.

You see, when we let fear dominate us, we lose the ability to come up with *ideas* because all our time is spent being afraid! We also lose our ability to gain perspective. We become myopic and thus don't see the solutions that we could use to fight off our fears. In my case a solution might have been to *practice* hitting with two strikes, or maybe to work on strike zone recognition so I could have become more confident in determining what was a strike and what wasn't. When we see through the eyes of fear we only see the fear. We're blinded to our *potential*, which unlike fear is boundless and eternal.

Now let's break down this hypothetical little league at-bat and look at a few scenarios that could have happened it if I didn't give in to my fear. By the time I waited for the best pitch to hit, the pitcher might have thrown a few balls! I might have been *ahead* in the count and thus transferred all the pressure over to the pitcher, which would have forced him to throw one right down the middle that I could have creamed. Or maybe the pitcher would have made two really good pitches for strikes that I wouldn't have hit well anyway, but on the third one I would have been looking to just make contact, which would have stopped me from over swinging, and would have given me a *better* chance for success. It's also possible that the same pitcher could have made a mistake on his third strike and left it out over the plate where I could have ripped the ball. As a consequence, my confidence would have soared off the charts because, not only would I have faced my fear, I would also have succeeded! And lastly, it's possible I would have struck out and realized I was going to have to work even harder to improve. And what's wrong with that? That's a valuable piece of information. But, regardless of the outcome, I would have gained precious bits of *character* that I could have spread throughout my whole life.

I wish I had been that kid and I wish I had had a coach or a father who could have guided me through those situations at that time in my life, but it was not meant to be. And that is not a rationalization on my part; I believe it to be true. I also believe baseball was meant to be more than just a lucrative career for me. It was a meant to be my teacher, my university, my shaman, my mentor and my way of understanding the seemingly random events of my life. And that is ultimately more important than being a professional baseball player. All one has to do these days is to take a look at the news to see many pro athletes, in various degrees of trouble, to know that success does not guarantee happiness...

When I was coaching my High School Baseball Team, I use to *make* my players take strikes and they'd often express their disdain with my methods because they didn't like being behind in the count. I was giving them fewer strikes with which to work and they didn't like the way it made them *feel*. They would say: "C'mon coach I can't hit with two strikes on me" or "It puts too much pressure on me; I always strike out". But I didn't relent because I knew there was more at stake than just a baseball game. They didn't know it then and they may never know it, but in my opinion it was their lives I was talking about not just hitting with two strikes on them. Someday they were going to face pressures far greater than an at-bat with two strikes and if they started running from their fears while in high school, they would never stop as an adult.

When I asked the kids to take strikes and go deep into the count I also asked them to do something else which *helped* them through the ordeal. I told them all I wanted them to do with two strikes was to make contact. That's it. I just wanted the ball somewhere out in the field of play. I felt that by giving them this instruction it was taking the pressure *off*. They didn't need to drive the ball into the gap or hit a homerun or do what most young players do, which is to try and kill the ball with every swing. Instead, I just wanted them to swing and to make contact, which made them stay *within themselves* instead of projecting a *false image* of themselves up at the plate that they could rarely live up to. The result at the end of the season was a confident bunch of hitters who finished the season 14-4, hit in the clutch, *with two strikes on them,* and beat teams they were getting crushed by the year before when they were freshman.

After the season was over, every player to a man said it was the best season they had ever had even though they didn't know why…"I can't explain it," they would say. "I just *felt* so confident. I just knew we were going to find a way to win." And to top it off one player said to me: "I never played that well in my life. For the first time I wasn't *afraid* to make a mistake because I *knew* I wasn't going to."

It's not every year that you get a group like the one I had that spring. Sometimes you can't get guys to buy into what you're trying to do. Maybe it was because that team had *no egos at all.* They were just a bunch of kids with average talent who loved baseball, liked each other and lacked confidence. It was just the kind of group that I love to coach. I'll take a bunch of kids who love the game and like each other over a bunch of talented, selfish and ego driven kids any day because those ego less kids are *open* and *trusting…*

So, if you're that hitter who is afraid, don't run from the fear. Listen to it. It's trying to tell you something important about yourself. It's giving you some insight into who you are. And if you look deep enough, it's also helping you to see *why* you are the way you are. And that is important! *That's why you're playing the game.* You're not playing just because you want to earn your letter or get your name in the paper or even to make the pros. You're playing baseball or studying to be a doctor or playing golf or raising a family or doing whatever it is you choose to do because life has meaning and it's your job to realize it.

Before I leave the God of Fear, I want to address one more thing. I have stated that people's fears are rooted in their low self-esteem. But, in reality, I think it goes much deeper than that. On the surface, succumbing to fear *does* relate directly to low self esteem and low self esteem *is* rooted in our childhood experiences, but when you probe fear to its deepest depths you find yourself asking the simple question: "What are we really afraid of?"

I would guess the answer for some would be that we are afraid of failure. But isn't it all how we look at failure? Aren't our failures sometimes our best learning experiences? I certainly know mine have been. After all how else can we learn? None of us are perfect so therefore failure is a valuable way for us to *grow* toward *perfection*. Otherwise we'd be perfect already wouldn't we? But all these questions aside, I think our fears are rooted in a place deeper than failure.

When we look at fear, being afraid of failure and the deflation of our self-esteem just doesn't seem to fit the raw power and magnitude of such an important God. Is the God of Fear just concerned with exposing our self-esteem? This is not to demean the importance of having self-esteem because lack of it can certainly make a shambles of someone's life. I'm living proof of that. But when we think of fear, what is the first thing that comes to our minds? Is it the fear of "striking out" in a literal and figurative sense? Or is it maybe the fear of not finding someone to love? Or on a grander scale not making of our lives what we had hoped for and dreamed of? *What are we really afraid of?*

It's possible that these real fears do pop up in our minds from time to time, but I believe the one thing we all fear more than anything else is our mortality, or maybe even worse that there is no God, no afterlife, nothing but us decaying six feet under the ground, with no hint that we were ever alive at all. That my friend is fear and that is where I believe the God of Fear wants us to go eventually when it enters our lives. It wants us to make that connection because it knows that only within this fear can we ever find an understanding about life! After all, how can we truly live a meaningful life if we have no understanding of death? It's like getting in a car and having no destination. There can be no journey, no life, without a destination. It is the destination that defines the journey.

Now you may be wondering why I bring up such a morbid subject in a baseball book? Well, for two reasons: The first is because so few ever talk about it. We stuff it somewhere in the deep recesses of our subconscious and only pull it out briefly when we either have a brush with death or some friend or family member dies. That's it. Then we stuff it back in again and try our best not think about it. But we don't realize that it colors everything we do in our lives.

The second reason is because talking about death here in this book or any-where for that matter adds *perspective* to our lives. If we can make our own mortality a part of our everyday lives then doesn't it make the tiny things we fear like hitting with two strikes a little less imposing? And maybe from that perspective we can relax, think clearer, make better decisions and play better baseball! I know it seems like a strange way of playing better baseball, but I never said the Baseball Gods were ordinary…

Now, you may be saying to yourself at this moment that you aren't afraid of death. Maybe you're strong in your faith and your belief in god and heaven. If that's the case then let me ask you these questions. "If someone came up to you tomorrow and put a gun to head would you be frightened?" Or if the plane you riding in suddenly began to plummet from the sky would you be scared? To a person, everyone I asked said he or she would be petrified even though they "believed" in God and that Heaven was waiting for them. But that answer is not logical. It makes no sense. Why wouldn't they be *looking forward* to going to "Heaven"?

When one examines all the major figures in the world's major religions one can see they were all trying to accomplish the same thing. They were all trying to conquer their fear of death. And, from what we have been told, they all achieved it. They were the trailblazers. They gave us the road map. But have we used it? Sure we've made great churches and temples, but what do they all *mean*? Those who are revered in these buildings did their work in the solitude of the mountains or the deserts with no fanfare and no audience. They didn't dress up in ornamental clothes or have fancy gold objects with them. They searched in their hearts and they found peace, which is the very thing I see lacking in today's world.

So what am I saying here? Should we all give up our lives and go live in the woods or wander in the desert? No, I'm not saying that. Even those major religious figures eventually came back to the world to live and teach *in* it. But what they did was they searched undistracted until they found. Now, whether or not you want to believe they found answers is up for debate. I think what they found were answers we can use as a guide to find our *own* answers.

I think baseball became my answer and there is a reason why it did. Because in spite of having so many painful childhood and teenage experiences, I continued to *love* baseball even when it wasn't giving anything to me, and that I believe is the key. Because when you love something, really love something; you give yourself over to it completely. There is no "*you*" anymore. You no longer have an ego or any desires or needs to be filled. You just *love*. And you expect nothing in return. You don't love this thing called baseball because you hope it will bring you something like fame or fortune. You don't love baseball because you need love back from it. You just flat out love it because of what it *is*.

Now, when I describe my love for baseball, it sounds like I'm describing something else doesn't it? It sounds like the love deeply religious people have when talking about God. And I ask you, are the two any different? I think to love baseball *is* to love God. How can there be any separation? Jesus said God is within everyone and everything and when he said that he wasn't excluding baseball because baseball is as real as anything else on this planet. To love baseball or anything with all of your being is to have a pure religious experience. The same kind every spiritual seeker has ever had. It is the same experience Jesus had while wandering in the desert or Buddha had while meditating on the Lotus Petal. It is losing oneself for the sake of loving something…

THE GOD OF ANGER

If you let the God of Fear dominate your life then you will also be at the mercy of its disciple, the God of Anger. Where fear dominates, anger is sure to be tagging along because that's people's natural reaction when faced with fear.

Fear paralyzes our ability to think rationally and to act with confidence. It tears down our self-esteem until, eventually, we find ourselves backed into a corner. And what happens when people are backed into a corner? They lose their rational ability and go into survival mode and that is when the anger comes out.

The expression of anger as a response to fear is natural in nature. Every species in the Animal Kingdom uses it to protect itself from life threatening situations as well as in circumstances that involve the setting of boundaries. Anger is usually quite effective in these scenarios and does provide the defense needed to fight off potential harm. In this way it is a necessary component essential to maintaining and preserving life as well as keeping it structured and orderly. But there is a warning. Anger is so effective in setting boundaries and protecting ourselves from harm that we are eventually *tempted* to use it in an offensive manner. And when we do, this is when we begin our downward spiral into darkness.

Human Beings feel anger when fearful or threatened and like animals we humans want to strike back, but unlike animals we, for the most part, don't. What we have done to inhibit the natural impulse to anger is to set up our society in such a way that it forces us to make the choice *away* from anger. We have done this by creating laws and penalties such as incarceration to inhibit the God of Anger's ability to function freely in our lives. This is our solution to the "Laws of the Jungle" that govern the rest of the Animal Kingdom. It was an ingenious invention and has represented a great leap forward in our attempt to elevate our species away from anger and toward peace. But living a civilized, peaceful life is often easier said than done.

There are many reasons why people get angry and in the last chapter I discussed one of the major reasons, The God of Fear. But it's not important whether it's the Gods of Fear, Ego or Self Esteem that triggers the God of Anger into action; what is important is that we *recognize* and *learn* from these Gods when they appear. Anger, Fear, Ego or many of the other gods I will discuss later are not malicious in their nature, even though we may manifest their energy in a negative way. On the contrary, the Gods are our teachers. They are trying to help us break through the veil of ignorance that we live under. It is this ignorance of the God's that causes us the pain, nothing else.

In the Animal Kingdom, anger is the main device used for the setting of boundaries. Animals and insects mark out their territory and then use various methods of intimidation to keep intruders away. This is how nature has set it up and it has worked extremely well. When a wolf marks off his territory with his urine he's telling you to stay out, and if you don't stay out then there will be trouble. There will be a war and you may be killed. It's harsh and it's violent and it's the law of the jungle.

Besides the setting and enforcing of boundaries, anger is also the last line of defense animals have against predators out to eat them for their dinner. In fact, many animals have natural anger response mechanisms set to fire when their senses detect they are in danger. The skunk for example has its hideous smelling spray that it uses to ward off attackers. The smell is so offensive to the attacking animal's olfactory systems that it debilitates it long enough so he can escape. It doesn't matter what kind of animal, insect or reptile it is one thing is for certain; it won't go down without a fight.

When people are afraid they become angry and this isn't *always* a bad thing, but it is an important sign that *something* is wrong. The expression of anger is a form of communicating to someone that you are being hurt or that your boundaries are being compromised and you *don't like it!* Believe it or not this is what the terrible twos are all about and it is vital that the correct lesson is taught at this important moment in the child's development. It is all how this expression of anger by the child is dealt with that determines its approach to anger for the rest of its life. We must respect the child's need for space and boundaries while at the same time teaching it to accomplish this goal without physical force. The problems come in when the expression of anger takes the form of physical violence or even verbal abuse by the parent, which subsequently lays down a violent foundation that is imbedded deep in the subconscious of the individual...

The game of baseball, as with any competition, can be the perfect setting for anger to appear. The reason for this is because games always involve conflicts of interest that mirror those we see in the animal kingdom. In sports there is always one player or team trying to invade another's defined boundary for the purpose of having it as its own. This struggle always involves some type of physical clash, which creates a breeding ground, similar to that of the jungle, where fear and anger can surface.

Since the inception of baseball there has been a never-ending struggle between the pitcher and the batter. The pitcher wants to claim certain sections of the plate as his own so he can be more effective in getting the batter out. The batter wants to block this domination and force the pitcher to throw the ball into regions of the strike zone more conducive for hitting.

The two regions of the strike zone the pitcher wants to control are the outside and inside corners. Conversely, the hitter wants to force the pitcher away from these areas and into the center of the zone. It is this eternal struggle, which sits at the center of the baseball universe. It is within this struggle where we see many gods, like the God of Anger at work.

The theory of pitching is that you pitch inside to set up the outside corner. If the pitcher can get the batter to concentrate on protecting the inside part of the plate because of the *fear* of either getting drilled by an inside pitch or by not being quick enough to get the bat head out, then he renders the hitter incapable of doing much with the outside pitch. It's one of the many fascinating intricacies of the game that make it a game of intellect rather than of brute force. Size just doesn't matter that much. If six foot ten inch Randy Johnson just throws his 95mph fastball right down the middle without setting batters up and working the corners he *will* get pounded. And on the flip side, the biggest and best hitters are always at the mercy of a pitcher of any size that can change speeds, work the corners and set up his pitches.

The pitching scenario I just described is one of the places where we see anger bubble to the surface. If a pitcher drills a hitter or even brushes him back, most of the time the hitter will just have a few choice words for the pitcher as he jogs down to first, But sometimes he may charge the mound and start a melee! It all depends on the level of anger inside both the pitcher and hitter.

When we analyze this situation from an energy point of view we see some interesting things at work. First we see the pitcher trying to gain dominance over the inside part of the plate and next we see the batter's reaction to that invasion of his space by charging the mound and trying to, in effect, reassert *his* dominance over the inside part of the plate. But what the combatants usually miss are the lessons doled out by the God of Anger.

The hitter and the pitcher sit atop a powder keg, which could blow at any moment, and it's how that potential for anger is dealt with that determines the at-bat as well as, if one wanted to stretch it out, the future enlightenment of the person. If the hitter lets the pitcher see he is angry then what he is telling the pitcher is that he *fears* something. Thus he makes himself *susceptible* to any number pitches, from off speed, to breaking pitches, to other inside fastballs. He's now emoting instead of being still. He is irrational instead of tactical and he is at the mercy of the pitcher and the God of Anger. Conversely, if the pitcher is throwing inside, with the *intention* to hit, because he is having a bad game or because a certain hitter "owns" him, then he is falling victim to the God of Anger as well and is actually showing a sign of *weakness* rather than strength. He is not winning his battle with the opposing team or the batter, but is instead *empowering* the other team because he's saying, by his anger, that he's not good enough to get the batters out with his skill. Ultimately, and more to the point, he's not winning the battle with himself either....

I've spent most of my baseball life as a pitcher and I've had numerous occasions where the God of Anger has gotten the best of me. I pitched in a Northeast Regional Tournament game in Maine recently where the umpire was blowing call after call. I mean everybody was yelling at this guy. Batters were cursing. I was cursing. The other pitcher was cursing. It was a scene that, if witnessed from a spectator's viewpoint, must have resembled a sand box with a bunch of two year olds fighting over a toy.

In the beginning of the game, I tried to not let it bother me. I would like to say I rose above it, but in reality what I was doing was *repressing* my anger. Not good. The God of Anger doesn't want to be repressed. It wants to be either dealt with in a healthy way with understanding or it wants to be heard so it can teach and enlighten. If it's repressed it just keeps knocking on the door harder and harder until it breaks it down in the form of *rage*.

As the game wore on, the blown calls began to pile up and I became a volcano about to blow. There wasn't a hint of positive energy left in my spirit. Also, at this time, another thing started to happen. My team started to screw up nearly every play behind me. And so, by the sixth inning and clinging to a 7-4 lead, I blew my top and lost complete control of what I was doing. I began to try to throw the ball harder and harder, which of course made it go slower and slower and with no control, and soon I began to pitch more like a petulant little leaguer and less like a forty two year old man who has had a long and successful career as a pitcher. Consequently, in the sixth inning, I was lifted from the game and came off the field full of rage. I kicked a cooler packed with ice and drinks and nearly broke my foot. Then I proceeded to lay blame in every direction imaginable except of course at myself. I was a raving maniac.

The game went on and our relief pitcher came in and closed it out and we hung on for the victory. Of course, he didn't have any of the problems I had with the umpire or with the fielding. Every play was made and every call was what it was, either a ball or a strike.

After the game was over, I drove back to Connecticut and I began to really *feel* what had happened out on the field. I had once again fallen victim to the God of

Fear, which led to the God of Anger, which led to me making a jackass out of myself.

As I discussed earlier in the book, I came into the 04' season pulling a boatload of negative energy behind me. I was depressed with my progress in life, professionally and personally, and wanted to keep the memory of my phenomenal 03' season in tact so I could salvage what was left of my long ago splintered self-esteem.

On that fateful day in Maine, I was representing Connecticut on a team that doesn't often lose (we have won many National and Regional Championships) and I was paralyzed with the fear of living up to my own reputation as one of the team's best pitchers. And so, armed with my sagging self-esteem and the fear of living up to my reputation, I took the mound in that game destined to self-destruct. I never really had a chance. My negative energy *drew* every bad call to me and made every ball hit find a place to land safely. And what was the result? Well you guessed it. All of my fears came to fruition and my sagging self-esteem crashed through the floor and shattered like stained glass into a million pieces.

To say I was at a low point in my life would be an understatement, but unlike when I was younger and unaware of the Gods, I could now realize that I had just had a major encounter with a Major God and I could try to learn something from the whole miserable experience. And what I learned was that I had to deal with my life long problem of Low Self-Esteem and to take action to change it.

What I had to realized and accept was that I was not like most people and that I never would be. I shouldn't condemn myself for my lack of material/professional success in this Western Culture I live in because the truth is I'm not a mainstream western person. I don't make mainstream art. I don't think mainstream thoughts and I'm probably never going to be on the cover of People Magazine and that's okay. My sights have always been set on something deeper whether I was pursuing my baseball career or my music career.

Fortunately or unfortunately, depending on whom you talk to, I've always seen life as a spiritual quest and I've seen the material world as symbols and metaphors that have helped to guide me in that quest. I don't think I've ever seen life literally although I've tried to pretend I have many times. I've always seen life figuratively and that doesn't always add up to material success. It may add up to that someday, but I hope I've made it clear in this book that it's the *meaning* that must come first if there is ever going to be happiness and peace in this world we live in...

Now, after our foray into the world of the powerful Major Gods, who shake us down to the core of our being, it's time to turn our attention to a different set of Gods called the Minor Gods. They sit on the surface of our consciousness and give us *hints* at the deeper issues affecting our lives. It's like when we were in school and the teacher told us to stop talking. What she was doing was giving us a warning shot. If we continued to talk we'd soon find ourselves in the principal's office and in *big trouble.* That's what the Minor Gods are; they're the warning shots that portend major disasters just around the corner...

The Minor Gods

There are Gods that are pre-eminent in the world we see around us. I called these the Major Gods. In Ancient Greece they lived on Mount Olympus and ran the show. In the game of baseball they represent the core energy that creates all the results we see quantified and qualified on the field. But, as with every ruling elite, they have assistants or minions who are delegated to handle the particulars and minute details that come with everyday life. I call these the Minor Gods. They are the external face of the internal and powerful energy of the Major Gods. They are the soldiers out in the field executing the battle plan laid down by the generals. But, even though I classify them as Minor, they are not to be taken lightly because like all soldiers they are tenacious. Remember, it wasn't the Generals who stormed the beaches at Normandy and drove the Germans out of France. It was the grunts out on the front lines. They are a lot less flashy in their approach and receive much less fanfare, but don't sell them short because if you do you will be missing a great opportunity to learn and to escape the fate doled out by the Major Gods. An analogy that comes to mind would be the addiction of smoking. When a new smoker decides to take his first drag on a cigarette he or she coughs and hacks violently because the negative energy of the smoke is invading the life giving positive energy of the lungs. That is the warning sign. That is the chance to say: "wait a minute, this is not good for me". But if the signs are ignored it ends up as a bad habit that is almost impossible to break and that also *kills*. So be careful not to underestimate these powerful Minor Gods because in some ways they are more important. They are out there on the front lines giving you the chance to fix the problem before it gets too big...

THE GOD OF CONTROL

If I had to dip into the Minor Leagues to pick out a God that has had a major influence on my life it would be the God of Control...

I've been a pitcher my whole life. I started pitching when I was ten years old and have continued to take the mound ever since. In all, I've been pitching on and off for thirty-two years. I've played other positions throughout the course of my career and I still play a decent third base on my men's league team, but it has been as a pitcher that I've carved out whatever identity I've had in the game of baseball.

You can ask any pitcher who's ever toed the rubber and he would agree there is one key ingredient needed in order to become a top-notch pitcher and that is control. A pitcher needs to be able to throw all his pitches, including off speed and breaking pitches, not just for strikes, but on the corners as well. I don't care who you are or how hard you can throw; if you don't have control you will eventually get tattooed. (Oh sure you will be able to get away with throwing the ball hard and right down the middle in High School and maybe even College, but when it comes to pitching against big time hitters you need to have the God of Control in your corner, appeased and happy.)

The importance of having control of your pitches cannot be over stated; it is everything. If you ask most pitchers what was the hardest thing they had to learn in their careers, ninety percent of them would say having great control.

The issue of control has always been on the front burner for me. As a kid, I could throw a ball through a brick wall, but I never had any idea where it was going. I remember a game when I was fifteen where I threw 248 pitches in seven-innings! I struck out 18 and walked 16! In another game I threw a no-hitter, but gave up four runs because I walked so many guys. I had no control at all, none. I've plunked so many batters in my career I'd need a calculator to add them all up.

I have had a life long relationship with the God of Control. It has been torturing me ever since I took the mound as a ten year old and it's only been within the last seven years that I've been able to send it off to haunt someone else. It hounded me doggedly for twenty-five years until I finally began to understand what it was trying to say to me. That's the one thing about these Gods. They will never go away until you face the music. They are tireless in their pursuit of the truth. So, if there is some pattern that has been continuously repeating itself during your lifetime, I would suggest you start looking for the God responsible. It's there. You just have to start looking at things from a different perspective in order to see it.

The pattern that had repeated itself over and over in my life was that I had control issues, not only while I was pitching in Little League, High School and College, but also in my personal relationships where I would let myself be controlled by others. It all added up to mess on and off the field.

Now, in keeping with the theme of this book, which is finding answers through the game of baseball, the question must be asked: What was the God of Control trying to tell me? Did it want me to just throw more strikes? Did it want me to practice more? Did it want me to work my mechanics more? Did it want me to shorten my stride or get on top of the ball? *What did it want?*

The God of Control wormed its way into every fiber of my being for a variety of different reasons, but none of them was to simply work on my mechanics. It could care less where my arm slot was or if I was striding in the right place. What it wanted me to do was to recognize that I couldn't throw strikes because I had control issues in my *life*. It wanted me to see that, in order to ever throw strikes and more importantly to have any chance at being happy, I had to *take control of my life.*

The reason why I couldn't throw strikes was because I grew up with a controlling and dominating mother and an overly critical father who sucked away my self-esteem by keeping me from expressing myself and finding my own individual nature. Consequently, I became lost and unsure and never knew where I fit in. I was so out of touch with myself that I felt like I was detached from my body. I lived exclusively inside my thoughts. My feelings were like foreign invaders. I felt them with great intensity, but I didn't understand them or had any connection to them. And when a person is completely disconnected from his feelings he is at the mercy of them. He is lost in the real world because he has no way of dealing with it. I spent much of my life a prisoner inside my head, isolated and alone.

It was in this depleted state that I would take the mound and try to pitch. It was like playing Russian roulette because I would never know what to expect. Some days the Gods would come calling and I would have no means with which to deal with them. The consequences would be chaos and walk after walk. Some days I would be okay because I would be feeling more secure at home and the Gods would leave me alone, but those days were few and far between. My life on the field was a reflection of the relationship I had with my parents and that was almost always full of stress and of course, control issues.

Now, I don't want to make it seem like I was an awful pitcher because I wasn't. Like I mentioned earlier, I was a Little League star and was one of the hardest throwers in the state as a high school pitcher. I also had many extremely successful moments in my college career and am in my college's Baseball Hall of Fame. But there is always a sense of regret that dwells inside me because I was never able to achieve what I was capable of achieving. Whatever I did achieve in baseball I did because of the force of my *will* and my *love* for the game *and* the love I had for my parents, in spite of the pain they were causing me. When a person loves something as much I loved baseball and my parents, he can fight through the effects of the Gods, but it's exhausting and eventually it's debilitating because the Gods are relentless. They drive at you like a hammer to a nail as long as the issues in question exist.

When I say that I have regrets and I talk about the pain that my parent's dominating attitude caused me, I only mean in terms of my material and egotistical success in the world of baseball. But the Baseball Gods, although concerned with improving my game, also see the big picture and are more concerned with you and me becoming successful in the *spiritual sense* as opposed to the *dollars and cents*! And so, in terms of life, the control issues I grew up with were important vehicles that I *needed* to lead me down the spiritual path. Again, it's all a matter of perspective. The worst things in life can become the best things if we look at life in terms of meaning. My childhood, though sad and painful, was *necessary* in order for me to find the Baseball Gods and that was *good* thing!

When I started this book I promised myself I was not going to focus on it being some kind of cathartic experience for me. I also didn't think it was necessary to air all the dirty laundry of my childhood because I wanted the book to be about *solutions*. But, as with most solutions in life, they come by means of trial and error. And so, if I'm going to talk of solutions, I have to show you the path that got me there.

Awful childhoods are only awful if they produce awful adult lives; otherwise they are valuable learning experiences. Everyone has their childhood issues because humans aren't perfect. For the most part people are frightened, unaware creatures just trying to survive under an extremely tenuous and uncertain condition called life. And my parents were no different. They couldn't use their past to find a solution to their present. But that doesn't mean I can't...

By the time I stopped playing competitive baseball I was twenty-two years old. I didn't get drafted to play professionally like I had hoped and then, after an attempt to play pro ball in Italy fell through, I tossed my glove and spikes into my father's garage and vowed never to play the game again. By twenty-two, I was so exhausted from my on going battles with the Baseball Gods that it was a relief to give it all up. I thought on some level that, if I didn't play baseball anymore, I would no longer be haunted by the inner sadness that had plagued me my whole life. But…I couldn't have been more wrong. The lack of control I always felt on the baseball field was now a lack of control in my everyday life. I spiraled downward in concentric and ever darkening circles. I began to drink and party heavily in order to escape the relentless attack of the Gods.

People always wonder why someone drinks too much or gets hooked on drugs, but when it's looked at in terms of the Gods it's easy to see. The drugs are an escape from having to deal with the omnipotent presence of the Gods in a person's life. When I drank I felt like the Gods were powerless. In fact, I laughed at them and taunted them. I felt free and powerful. I had found a source of energy stronger than the Gods called alcohol. Of course, that power was only there when I was drinking because the next day they'd be right there at my bedside poking and prodding at me trying to get me to wake up from my ignorant slumber. But I didn't want to wake up from that slumber. Who the hell really wants to? To wake up means to face one's problems and who wants to do that? It's so much easier to live in denial and drown myself in the material world than it is to look for meaning. And the great thing is that you will have lots of company in your material pursuit of denial. Most of the world lives this way.

After I quit playing ball, I stumbled and bumbled for the next thirteen years and tried my best to escape the Gods in whatever way I could. But, for me, there would be no escape because no matter how hard I tried I could never push back that one lone voice in my soul that said that life had meaning. So, slowly and without knowing consciously what I was doing, I began to piece together the feelings I was having and relating them to similar feelings I had had in the past. What I was beginning to do was to listen to the Gods. And they had a lot to say…

My thirteen-year exile from the game took me in many different directions. Over that time I began a career in music and purged my feelings out in songs. I read every book on spirituality and psychology I could get my hands on and studied it Graduate School. I drove across the country ten times and slept in my car while I wrote in my journal. I meditated and did Yoga and nearly lost my life in a bicycle accident in Los Angeles. I read books on Mythology and Astrology and scoured the earth for the answers to questions that I was only dimly aware of, but that I couldn't deny. Then, after years of trial and error, I had finally begun to put my life back together when, from out of the blue, a fateful call arrived from my old college teammate that I hadn't seen or talked to in years. He wanted to know if I was interested in playing baseball in a men's over thirty league?

At first I was reticent and quite frankly afraid. I wasn't sure if I could return to that painful place of long ago. But, going on my gut feeling, I said yes anyway because a part of me could feel myself coming full circle, and I didn't want to miss the opportunity to close the circle. I accepted the invitation to the old battlefield of my youth and a funny thing happened when I got back on the field. I felt like a kid again. And another thing happened too, I saw the Baseball Gods for the first time and I began to listen to what they had to say. It didn't take me long to realize my search for answers was over. I was back where I belonged. I had found my temple and now it was time to pray.

What I had done in those thirteen long years away from the game was to take control of my life. I began to build a foundation under myself for the first time and began to give myself all the things my childhood had lacked. I had gained a better understanding of who I was and where my place was in the world. What I did in effect was to become my own mother and father and to grow myself up, only correctly this time. I started to allow my individuality to be validated and I began to believe in myself. I expressed myself honestly and without shame. I didn't always make good decisions, but I found wisdom in them instead of shame. I began to feel love and more importantly I didn't want to settle for anything short of love in my life again. And guess what happened? When I took the mound again I had *control!* I threw strike after strike after strike and the bells began to go off. I knew why I was throwing strikes. It was because I was in control of my life and that control became control on the mound. One strand of the circle had been reconnected and I felt a sense of being complete…at least for a while. Soon I began to see that there were many, many more strands to be reconnected and many more Gods to face, hellish gods that have taken me to hell and back, but who have always left me with a feeling of getting closer to love. And that makes it all worthwhile…because love is all I ever really wanted.

I'd like to make one last comment on the God of Control before I move on. Everyone who has a control issue doesn't necessarily have the same one that I have. There are some people who are not *out of control* but *in control* of everything and everyone around them. For these people being too perfect and expecting that perfection from everyone is his or her problem. They are the micro managers and the Felix Unger's of the world and they have control problems, but just from the opposite side.

The player who tries to control everything and everyone is much like the ego player. He will perform to the highest of his ability and will unquestionably be successful, but unfortunately for him he won't enjoy it. He won't allow himself to be vulnerable because being vulnerable also means he might feel pain and he can't handle that. Pain means dealing with the reason why he is a control freak and that is a place he doesn't want to go. He takes everything on his shoulders because he believes he is the only one who can do it right. He doesn't empower people because deep down he isn't secure enough inside to have anyone be his equal. He appears strong, but in reality he's weak and afraid and so he compensates for this by domination. This way, he feels, he can hide his true self from the world.

There are various conditions under which the controller controls. He can do it physically, emotionally or spiritually. But, despite the kind of control being asserted, the solution is *always* the same. The way to deal with a controlling person is easy. You don't let him control you. You remove yourself from the situation. The controlling person needs someone to control. Without it he or she is powerless. There's no use trying to be rational because the controlling person is *irrational* in his relations with people. The best thing to do is to remove oneself from the situation and hope that within the ensuing silence some type of epiphany may take place that will help the person see the light. Silence, after all, is what every spiritual seeker uses to find God. But the bottom line for *you* is that you are aware of the situation and you deal with it in a way that keeps your energy intact. Because remember, a person who is a controller needs someone to control and he has targeted you as the type of person that *can be controlled*.

The issue of control comes up often in the relationships we have. In fact, I think it would be safe to say that all healthy relationships involve some kind of back and forth until there is a balance reached. I also think it would be safe to say that very few relationships ever find that balance. Again, it is our attachment to the material world, which the culture has decided is devoid of meaning, which prevents it.

The world seems to be divided into three types of people. Those that are only concerned with being in control of their own lives, those that are just interested in controlling other people and those that let themselves be controlled. Of the three the latter two are the most common and the former is seemingly non-existent.

The energy of control is closely tied to the energies of the ego and self-esteem. If you are one who is weak and easily controlled then you *lack* the self-esteem to stand on your own two feet and are looking for someone to hold you up. What you must do is go back to your childhood and look forward to see the patterns and the areas of your life that are vulnerable. Then you must shore them up. You must learn to support yourself. There is nothing wrong with being sensitive and open, but it must be balanced out with strength and resolve. (As a side note, there are those that over give and worship their partners as a way to control *them*. They know that the controller's ego needs to be fed and so they feed it thereby making the controllers think they are in control when really they're being manipulated. It's all very complicated and such a waste of energy!)

If you are the controller then you also suffer from low self-esteem, but you've learned to compensate for it by inflating your ego and adapting a domineering presence. To keep the ego inflated and the image of yourself intact you need to find low self-esteem people that you can control with fear or that you can "save" thus ensuring a lifetime worth of worship. But you mustn't settle for this autocratic life. You too must look back and find out what it is that you're afraid of and you must face it. You must find out what fears you are compensating for with control so you *can become vulnerable.* This what you are here for, what we are all here for, to face the truth about ourselves so we can make changes. Otherwise the Gods will torture you forever.

On the baseball field, the difference between a player who is in control of his actions and one who is a controller is that the person in control of himself is relaxed and is a leader. He knows who he is and what he can do and he leads by example. He doesn't tell teammates what they should do. He tries to educate them on what is best for the *team.* He knows that for any partnership to work, be it teammates or relationships, it takes every man being empowered rather than controlled. He is a person who is neither too open nor too closed. He sits directly in the middle and is both at the same time because he knows the two must work together in unison, just like the front side that leads the body during the pitching motion, but then gives way to the backside as it follows through—like the bottom hand that leads the swing toward the ball, but then gives way to the top hand at the moment of contact during the swing. And lastly, like the opposing muscles in our bodies that constantly contract and flex in order to keep us in perfect balance...Being in control is about being in balance and that leads me to our next god...

THE GOD OF BALANCE

The game of baseball cannot be played with any degree success without being in tune with the God of Balance. It doesn't matter whether you are pitching the ball, hitting the ball or fielding the ball, balance is essential if you are going to do it correctly.

When a pitcher goes through his wind up he reaches a place called the *balance point*. It is here that his arms and legs get into the right position to drive toward the plate and release the pitch. If a pitcher (say right handed) is falling forward at the balance point, he will deliver the ball either high and inside or low and away (to a right handed batter). The effect of being out of balance will cause him to compensate by tucking his elbow in, which will make his arm trail behind thus causing the ball to go high and away, or it will force him to rush his arm through causing him to yank the pitch down and away. The same can be said for the pitcher who is out of balance by leaning too far back at the balance point. His pitches will also go high and inside or low and away.

If you were to film the perfect pitching motion and then break it down frame by frame you would see perfect balance at every point. As the left arm reaches toward the plate, the right arm reaches back away from the plate. As the left arm pulls down, the right arm raises up. As the left side lands, the right side pushes off. For every action there is an equal and opposite reaction (Newton's third law of motion) all in perfect balance. At least that is the idea.

If we switch to the batter's box the issues are similar. A batter must be in balance if he is to have the best chance of hitting the ball square and hard. Although, a hitter can be woefully out of balance and still manage to flair one to the outfield for a hit, or dribble one in the infield for a hit. But that being said you will never get the point of being even an average high school player if you don't have some degree of balance in the box.

Much like the pitcher, if a batter is lunging forward at the ball he will not hit it square. He will either pop it up or hit a routine grounder that is right at someone 90% of the time. If he is leaning back, dropping his shoulder and collapsing his back leg, he is destine to hit one lazy fly ball after another.

In my many years as a coach, I have found problems with balance to be one of the most prevalent I've encountered. It seems like all I'm ever doing is reminding the pitcher not rush or the batter not to lunge.

The reasons why young players are constantly out of balance are usually pretty simple. It is because they are being affected by any number of Gods like low self esteem, fear, anger, anxiety, impatience, hesitance, trying too hard, frustration, lack of confidence or numerous other inhibitions that encompass the full spectrum of energy that we call teenage life. As a high school coach, I've always been keenly aware that, at all times, there are a bevy of gods wreaking havoc on a teenager's life, on and off the field. I am also aware it is my job not to *solve* every energy problem, because that is impossible and can only come from within the person, but instead to inject *my energy* into the situation, which I hope will help him see what he is *capable of.*

What I try to do when my players are having balance problems or any baseball problems is to shift the focus away from mechanics and toward the energy I believe is causing the disturbance. I try to accomplish this by crawling inside their heads and hearts and working with their energy problems from the inside out. I do this by repeating commands like a mantra on a pitch-by-pitch basis. It's like I'm the training-wheels constantly keeping the whole thing balanced until their confidence can emerge and they can ride on their own. The ballplayer's balance problems are not going to be fixed by placing a foot here or an elbow there, but by changing the energy *causing* the body to fall out of balance and out of place.

The reason why I take this approach is three fold. First off, the constant sound of my voice focuses the player and his run away emotions on me and only me. This calms him down, removes the Gods temporarily from the picture and allows him to perform correctly. Next, it gives him a glimpse into the world of focus, through my eyes, that he might not ever have had before. And lastly, it lets him know what his potential can be. If you give a child a taste of candy he always wants more and if you give a young ball player a taste of success, where his body is in tune with his spirit, then he might become hungry for more and begin to search inside his own heart for answers.

I learned this method from a coach I had when I was in my teens and playing American Legion Baseball. He had me pitching in perfect balance, perfect control and without fear. I never used to walk batters when I pitched for him. He crawled inside my head and became my balance, my control and my confidence. All I heard during the game was his voice. It was as if I were being hypnotized. I was getting was a taste of what baseball was like when the Gods were out of the way and it made a lasting impression on me...

As I progressed through baseball, I never forgot the success I had under his tutelage even though I didn't understand it. But I do now. What he did was to get my teammates and me to buy into his vision and to leave the Gods up to him. He didn't specifically refer to the Gods the way I am doing right now because for him it was more of a visceral approach, but it didn't matter because the results were sensational for us. Collectively, we never played better baseball than we did when we played for him and on that team.

Now, on the surface, it might appear like he was brainwashing us or controlling us, but it was much more than that. We were young and inexperienced and were not prepared to deal with the Gods. We needed someone to guide us through the rough seas. That's what mentors and or parents are *supposed to do!* They're supposed to supply us with a glimpse of what we *could be* and *that* is important, because it gives us all something to shoot for. It makes us see that we can achieve more than what we thought we were ever *capable of* achieving by taking *fear out of the equation.*

What he did, in effect, was to show us that, although we had issues, we were capable of conquering those issues. Sure he was in our heads, but we still had to perform and when we did it gave us a confidence we didn't know we could have. You can't see where you're capable of going unless you can get a glimpse of it. He provided that glimpse and then it was up to us to take the journey and fulfill our potential.

There was one other lesson he taught us in those three years of summer ball back in the late seventies. He taught us about the God of Trust, which may be one of the most important of all the lessons to learn. You see, when he asked us to trust him with our baseball ability, he was showing us how important it was and is to trust other people, because nothing great has ever been achieved without trusting others. Everything in life is done as a team because after all, we are all here on this planet together. When we trusted him and succeeded we began to trust each other and became *one team* instead of a collection of individuals. We were no longer afraid to give ourselves over to another person. We gave our trust to each other and so each person had the strength of the whole team behind him instead of just trying battle *alone.* (Every now and then I run into one of those guys and it doesn't matter how much time has passed because we are all still bound by that experience. To each other we are all still teenagers woven together within a fabric called love, which is and will always be timeless and eternal…)

I'd like to end this discussion of the God of Balance by saying one thing that directly relates this humble God to the field of action. To be balanced on the field is exactly as it sounds. You must have a solid base and be steady at all times. All your muscles must work together to keep you on an even keel throughout your windup or batting stance. It must be remembered though that there is no "right" way to get that balance for *all people.* There is no "right" pitching motion or "right" batting stance. On the contrary, you must *discover* what *feels right for you!*

As I've said before, there are as many different ways to achieve balance, as there are souls on earth. You'll know you've got it when it *feels right*. Then it's up to you get to know that feeling until it becomes a *way of pitching*, and ultimately a *way of life*…

When we are working with young kids or teenagers the chances of making an impact on their balance problems are good. Their lives are still relatively uncorrupted and their ideals are still somewhat intact. But what about when we are dealing with adults, with all their complications, exploded ideals, dashed dreams and mountains of baggage? What can an adult do when dealing with balance issues?

When an adult's life has become unbalanced it is because one or more of the Major Gods has taken over his life and has led him down a path dominated by the material world. What he needs to do is to even out the scales.

When an adult player's self-esteem is low or is in the grips of fear he tends to look for answers within his culture to bail him out. In western culture he thinks he needs to hit more homeruns, become richer, have more possessions, an exciting affair, get another degree or do anything that will feed his ego and thus raise his self esteem. Unfortunately, this is all that western culture can offer him and from the looks of our crumbling unbalanced social structure it isn't nearly enough.

A person living an unbalanced life needs to examine it and find the areas that are tipping the scales; then he must make changes. He must stop gorging himself on the material world and begin to feed himself a diet rich in the spiritual as well. If, for example, he is a workaholic then he must examine what God is driving him (probably the Gods of Fear and Control) to work in exclusion of other things in his life and he must begin attending to those people or things he is forsaking. If he is someone who is a painfully shy person then he needs to find his external voice. If he is a selfish ball player he needs to become more selfless. If he only pulls the ball then he needs to learn to hit the other way.

We all have varying degrees of unbalanced feelings in our nature and it's vital that we balance them off. We will never free ourselves from the Gods if we don't find balance. Our unbalanced nature will leave us just one step ahead or behind in our search for peace of mind and true love…

What the subject of balance also brings to mind is the connection between balance and disease. Eastern medicine makes a strong connection between the balance of energies in the body and illness. This is what Acupuncture, Meditation and Chiropractics is all about and they are extremely effective. There are also more fringe medicines like Reiki and Aroma Therapy that focus on the Chakras or energy centers in the body and they have been effective as well.

The concept of balance isn't just confined to the area of health; it is valued everywhere in our culture. In Washington D.C. they talk of the need for a Balanced Budget even though they rarely accomplish it. Then there is the Balance of Power ingeniously built into our democracy by our founding fathers. It is this balance, which separates our form of government from most throughout the world. Next, we have the Balanced Diet, which extols the virtues of eating the right foods in the right amounts to create a healthy body. In science we have Newton's Third Law of Motion that I mentioned earlier, which states: "For every action there is an equal and opposite reaction". See how it works? When things are balanced they work better and more efficiently whether it's the government, the earth or you....

The Gods in Waiting

In the first part of the book I focused on the Gods that most people would recognize. They consisted of omnipotent deities who wielded a great deal of power and energy and whose lessons hit to the core of the player's very soul. I called them the Major Gods.

In part two, I covered the Minor Gods who, although powerful in their own right, still served as subordinates to the Major Gods. I described the Minor Gods as the outer layer in front of the deep, dark Major Gods who are responsible for putting out subtle signs that point us toward the major lessons we need to learn.

But now, I want to look at another set of Gods who, on the surface, don't seem all that powerful, but who can be of great influence if they are tapped into. I call them the *Gods in Waiting*.

The Gods in Waiting are valuable tools for unlocking the treasure trove of positive energy within us all. They have the potential to *fix* the problems of the past.

Up until now I have been facing the Major and Minor Gods head on and slugging it out with them. I have delved deep into my own memories and probed my own subconscious to give you a picture of what you are up against. I haven't painted a pretty picture, but then again the path toward self-awareness has never been an easy one. It's not easy to let go of one's belief that the material world is reality. But there are Gods out there to help make the trip a little bit more bearable and that's what I'd like to concentrate on now. It's time to *find solutions*.

If you listen to anyone in athletics these days they'll mention the need for things like focus, intensity, confidence, attitude, composure, patience and trust, but no one ever says how you get these things. You're just supposed to have them!

So far I've looked at the Major and Minor Gods and showed how they expose our many weaknesses and also how they set up road blocks and detours on our road to success on and off the field. I've also talked about how we must face these issues at their source, our childhood, as way to overcome the improper energy and programming we received as children. To do this we must change our *perspective* away from the material/mind/matter reality and toward the invisible/feeling/spiritual reality of energy, which according to science, religion *and* art *is* the true nature of reality. I've empathized with everyone's arduous journey, but have promised an increased awareness and inner contentment, as well as an increased ability to play baseball if you attend to these Gods and to reality in this way. The one thing I haven't done is to give you any tools to help you along the way. Now it's time to open up the toolbox.

From my years of playing and coaching, I have discovered numerous Gods just waiting there to help you if properly contacted. That's why I call them the *Gods in Waiting*. They aren't going to hover around you and get in your face like the other Gods. They're only going to bestow their graces on those who will recognize and worship them. After all, isn't that why we worship Gods so they will bestow some grace on us? What would be the point of worshipping God if there weren't a heaven waiting at the end of our pilgrimage?

THE GOD OF REPETITION

The first God in Waiting I'm going to cover is one that is grossly underrated, because of its lack of flash, but is extremely good at what it does. I know it's going to be a hard sell in this twenty first century of fast foods, quick edits, ADHD and excessive desire for the "next big thing", but I have to try anyway. The God I'm talking about is the God of Repetition.

Now, I can hear you saying: *The God of Repetition? What the heck is he talking about? How is that going to help? How bout the God of Good Luck or the God of Steroids or maybe even the God of Technology? How about them? The God of Repetition? Get lost pal! Go and sell your wares to someone else. We want answers, not more problems!*

Well, I know from his humdrum title it doesn't seem like this God can be of much help, but it is just the opposite. In fact, the God of Repetition just might be the most powerful "God in Waiting" there is.

When I coached my High School team we would do an infield drill called "four corners". The point of this drill was that each infielder was paired up with someone specifically designated to him ground balls. The fielders would man their positions while other players would position themselves along the first and third base lines and hit ground ball after ground ball to the fielder. The theory behind this exercise was to give the fielder an opportunity to field a hundred or so groundballs, while at the same time helping to increase the batter's eye/hand coordination. It was an exceptional example of repetition…when it was done correctly.

The purpose of all practice drills whether they are for fielding, hitting or pitching is to repeat an action over and over so it can become something that a player doesn't have to *think about*. Taking the mind out of the picture and leaving it to do what it does so well, which is to analyze and interpret data and to coordinate the systems of the body, is the key to performing well on and off the field. And that is the whole point of the God of Repetition.

Practicing a skill over and over puts the player in the heart of the Zen state I discussed earlier, wherein the player's movements become instinctual and he is one with the game. He doesn't think about what he has to do he just *does it*. He doesn't feel fear when the ball is hit to him; he *is* the ball hit to him. He isn't afraid of whether or not he will hit the ball when he is at-bat; he *is* the pitch thrown to him. There is no separation.

Because of his worship of the God of Repetition, the player in this Zen like state sees the game move as if it were in slow motion. When everyone else is frantic, he is in step with the play. When the game is tense and the players are tight, he is relaxed and not fighting the action, but instead is *flowing* with it.

As a player, I practiced and practiced endlessly and I believe that is the reason why I was able to over come the emotional problems I was having at home. The repetition I did on and off the field gave me an increased ability to focus, which balanced out the devastating effect the Major and Minor Gods were having on me.

Another positive effect of my dedication to the God of Repetition was that I was also able to maximize my baseball abilities from a body, which was far from athletic. When I look back today I'm amazed I was able to consistently be the best player on the field despite being gangly, uncoordinated and with no self-esteem.

The God of Repetition can be as powerful as any God in the baseball world, but it is a God that most players, especially today, are reluctant to tap into. Granted it is demanding and is not for the feint of heart, but once you turn your life over to it then it becomes an empowering force with few if any peers.

Unfortunately, what I have found with most of today's young players is that when I've used repetitive practice techniques it dissolves into boredom, which then leads to sloppiness and a breakdown of the drill. But the breakdown of the drill doesn't matter to me because I do the drills for two reasons. The first is to help sharpen the skill level and awareness of those players who *are* dedicated and have what it takes to learn from the Gods. And secondly, to *expose* those whose character might not match their skill level.

There are numerous reasons the God of Repetition is so demanding on its disciples. For a player to fully feel the benefits of this stern God he must deal with boredom and isolation. He must let go of his *ego* because no one applauds while one is working with this God. And lastly, he must deal with the issue of time, because the magic effects don't take hold right away. There has to be an enormous amount of time invested. The God of Repetition pays off in the *long run*, not in the *short term*. And in today's quick fix, fast food world, where young people's ability to focus has been altered by the culture's edited pace, the God of Repetition has barely gotten a sniff. So it lays dormant just waiting there for someone to come along and to tap into its awesome power.

Today's world seems to be the antithesis of the God of Repetition. Why should we watch what we eat and exercise to lose weight when we could take a pill, get liposuction or have our stomach stapled? Why should we hone our skills and build the muscles we need to perform through hard work when we can get them artificially through steroids? Why should we take the time to find out why we are depressed when we can take a drug that puts the smile back on our face? Why should we learn to do anything when we can pay someone else to do it? These are the theme songs of the twenty first century and they are stripping us of our soul.

The God of Repetition knows that it's boring. It knows that it requires you to spend many hours alone in order to strip away the roadblocks put up by the other Gods. It knows that it's going to force you to give up wasting time having self-indulgent "fun" because you have to practice. But it also knows that in the end you will get more of a return on your investment than in any other endeavor you will attempt. And that is because you will be investing in yourself. You will be getting a return called *self worth*, which is the cornerstone of happiness and can't be bought because it is priceless.

I know the power of the God of Repetition because I have felt its impact in many different areas of my life. Like I said earlier it was the main force that kept me from being destroyed by the other Gods. Also, another of its great qualities is that it's always there to tap into no matter how old you might be. So if you're struggling with your life or just want more from it, tap this noble God on the shoulder and do what it wants you to do. You won't be sorry…

THE GOD OF ACCOUNTABILITY

There hasn't been a bigger and more overused buzz word in the last five years than the word accountability. The reason for this overexposure is simple. It's because so few are accountable these days! It's also become blatantly obvious that the lack of accountability is at the heart of many of today's problems.

In my work with young players the biggest challenge I face is to get them to take responsibility and be accountable for their results. It's always the umpire's fault or the coach's fault or the sun's fault for being in the sky. It is never their fault. One might say the lack of accountability is the theme song of this current generation. This is not to say that others have *nothing* to do with your pain, because it is more than possible that another person is inflicting some of his or her issues on you. But the question is why did you draw this negative energy to yourself? And what was your part in the play that just unfolded? Remember, your energy determines the outcome of any situation in your life. If you are on the receiving end of someone's anger or ignorance, I guarantee you that you drew this energy to you for some reason that only you know and to ignore that is to miss to lesson.

In the introduction I talked about this phenomenon as being one of the main inspirations for this book. I discussed how things always seem to go wrong for the team that doesn't pay attention to the gods. The umpires always seem to blow calls at the worst possible times and the bad hops always seem to find their way into the play you need most. For page after page, I've been introducing you to the Gods you will meet when you *don't* have any accountability.

I have come to understand throughout the years, although at times I've come to it kicking and screaming, that I am responsible for everything that happens to me. If an umpire is squeezing me then I brought this to me in order to learn a lesson. Maybe it's a test to see how well I can overcome adversity. Maybe it's a test for my self-esteem or my anger. But whatever the Gods have in store for me it is my job to deal with it right there or else suffer the consequences. Sometimes I do and sometimes I don't. And when I don't, I suffer and lose the game. When I do, I succeed. But either way I end up learning because, after the game is over and my *emotions* have calmed, I inevitably begin to *feel* and then understand.

Now, even if *I am* in touch with the gods during a game, that doesn't mean we, as a team, are going to win or that things won't go wrong around me. Everyone else on the field has their own energies to cope with and they are out of my control. All I can do is my best and hope that my energy can either overcome or *aid* whatever my teammates might be struggling with on that day. The key is how

I *deal with it.* If I start to point fingers then that's not going to help. It will only add more negative energy to an already bad situation. But if I show confidence in myself and have no fear of losing then maybe it *will* have a positive effect on the team and will help to turn things around. It's not that I can *change* their energies, but I can *inspire them* to change it for themselves. It all starts with accountability.

One of the best examples of dealing with negativity is a situation where a fielder makes a key error to let in the tying run in a close game. I've seen it happen more times then I'd care to remember and it is a perfect time to see how the other players and more importantly the pitcher reacts to the God of Accountability. The pitcher, for example, has a choice. He can become *angered* by it and spew negative energy or he can try to pick up his teammate by having the confidence enough to know that he can get the next guy out. If he chooses to remain positive the chances are he *will* get out of it. But if he chooses to point the finger of blame well then...

I was pitching a game this past year against our arch rivals and there was no score going into the fifth inning. The game was for first place and the intensity was high. Everyone knew it was going to be a low scoring game where every play could swing the game one way or another. The inning started off well with me getting the first out via a strikeout. Then the next batter, a lefty, came up and hit a ball just slightly to the left of our centerfielder. When the ball was hit I was confident that I had the second out, but when I turned around I noticed that our centerfielder was playing way over toward right field and couldn't make the catch. I immediately became angry because, in my opinion, he had failed to position himself correctly and then he compounded the mistake by fumbling the ball as the hitter raced to second. When the play was finally over I was dejected, angry and full of fear because I knew what a costly play it was. We weren't hitting well and one run was probably going to decide it. I was setting myself up for defeat.

On other days I would have shaken the whole thing off and would have been confident they weren't going to get a run off me. But on this day I let it get to me. I decided at that moment that this was going to be just another lousy experience of what had been a lousy stretch of time in my life. So, of course, what do you think happened? The next guy lined a base hit to score the run.

But it didn't end there. After the run scored, I regained my composure and realized that I had to keep it at one run. I convinced myself that I was throwing the ball well and that we could get a couple of runs off their tough pitcher. I was listening to the Gods and so consequently, I calmed down and proceeded to get the next guy to ground out. I could feel the momentum beginning to swing back in my direction. The next batter stepped in and he was a guy I felt for sure couldn't hit me. I had had great success against him in the past and so...*I took it for granted* that I would get him out. Mistake. I had gone from confident to over confident. I proceeded to get two strikes on him, which over inflated my cockiness even more, and then on the third pitch I just rolled a curve ball up to the plate and actually started to lean toward the dugout fully expecting him to take it for strike three. But, as I began to shift my mind away from the moment and toward the bottom half of our inning, he stuck out his bat and just poked a little flair out to left field. Now, because there were two outs, the runner on second was moving on contact and so he figured he could score on the hit even though it was barely past the infield dirt. My left fielder raced in and picked up the ball and had the runner dead to rights at home by at least ten feet. But once again I had a feeling of dread...

As the throw left his hand I could feel myself expecting the worst. I turned back toward the plate to see the result and watched as the throw went way off the mark, bouncing past the catcher and to the backstop, with the run scoring easily. Once again, the first thought in my mind was that the team had failed to make a play behind me. I didn't see that he was giving it his all and doing the best he could. I was only thinking of the fact I was going to lose to a team that I needed to beat in order to inflate my sagging self esteem. But what I should have been thinking of was the fact that I had *failed to see* how lightly I had taken the hitter in the first place! Instead, I became enraged inside and completely lost my focus, failing to see that if I could just get the *next* batter out we would only be behind 2-0.

With anger and blame and no accountability pumping through my veins, I proceeded to try and throw the next pitch as hard as I could and what do you think happened? You guessed it. I threw the ball right down the middle, belt high and with no movement. Result? The batter smacked a two run homer to make it 4-0, which effectively put the game out of reach.

After the game, I was disappointed in myself because of my inability to handle my self-esteem issues after the miscues. I was also disgusted in myself for my lack of accountability. There were no excuses for my lapses in awareness. But, even if I thought there were excuses, the Gods didn't want to hear them anyway. They just wanted to make their point and hopefully make a big enough impact on me to drive their lessons home.

I guess the point of me sharing my own struggles with the Gods is to illustrate the fact that, even though I'm the writing this book and trying to communicate with the Gods on a daily basis, the journey is never complete. There is no end of the road where the learning stops. There is no graduation. Everyday of our lives is filled with challenges and surprises that we could never have anticipated and all of these challenges and surprises test our ability to handle the Gods...

Many people I know complain of being in a rut in their marriage or trapped in a dead end job or frustrated by their lack of material success, but they don't realize how good they really have it, how lucky they really are. So they waste their lives feeling sorry for themselves or making excuses or blaming others. But what they don't know is that the Gods are always listening and they will tap into their weakness and really give them something to feel bad about. The Hindu's call it Instant Karma. Remember the energy you have inside you is a powerful thing. It attracts the Gods who will then do what they have to do to get you to become accountable...

So do yourself a favor right now and stand up and try to become 100% accountable for where you are in your life. Don't be afraid. I know you think your self-esteem can't handle being wrong, but it can. And believe it or not the more you face up to your end of the accountability rainbow the better you will feel about yourself and the less problems you will have! Also, a funny thing will happen when you do hold yourself accountable. People around you will follow suit and do the same. They won't let you shoulder 100% of the blame. They will insist on taking at least 50% from you. Soon you'll find yourself in the position of being a leader and having better interpersonal relationships than you ever had before. You'll also find yourself happier as well. The God of Accountability is one great God to have on your side. He can be a taskmaster like the rest of the Gods, but he also has the power to free you from your self-made purgatory if you let him. (But just one warning...Don't be accountable for something unless you really *mean it* because the consequences are worse by ten fold if your humility is false. You will not only lose your credibility, you will never be trusted again and you will incur the wrath of one pissed off and powerful god.)

I'd like to make one final note about accountability before I move on to our next God in Waiting. People often think that being accountable is saying that they're sorry or, as I hear out the field, players saying "My Bad" when they make an error. But these *words* are not what the God of Accountability is looking for out of you and me.

I have a rule on my team. No player is ever allowed to say: "My Bad" or "I'm Sorry" for a blunder. I say to them: "We all know it's your bad and that you're sorry for your mistake, but what we want to hear you say is that you know *why* you threw it to the wrong base, or let it go through your legs, and that it *won't happen again!*"

You see, players (especially young players) think that the apology or admission of guilt *absolves* them from taking any further action. They feel that all they have to do is to say these words and they're free to blunder again. I had one kid back when I first started coaching who made three errors in a row in a game and after everyone he said: "My Bad". I couldn't believe what I was hearing. And so after the inning was over I asked him why he made three errors in a row and he had no answer for me. He hadn't learned a thing. His admission was all he thought he needed to do. He didn't know he was supposed to learn anything!

THE GOD OF TRUTH

Of all the Gods in Waiting, the God of Truth is quite possibly my personal favorite. This is because of its paradoxical nature. It is both extraordinarily complicated and refreshingly simple and direct at the same time. Also, it is by far the least understood, most misquoted God in the history of mankind. And unfortunately it is the reason given for every awful thing that has ever happened anywhere and at anytime.

Often people think that social institutions like religion and science are to blame for all of man's deviant behavior, but that is not the case. It is man's inability to understand what the God of Truth is saying that has led to the problems we see in our own lives, as well as in the world around us. And you can take it from me, the God of Truth is not happy about it.

At this point, you may be asking yourself why I would make such a sweeping indictment of the human race when it comes to the God of Truth, but if you stop and think about it, every deviant behavior, every war and every single disagreement is because of a clash of incongruous truths. For example, Hitler believed his statements about the superiority of the Aryan race to be true despite how insane they were. He felt his persecution of the Jews to be a truth, and so he murdered them.

We see many attempts to justify murder like this on a daily basis. We see religions entrenched in their dogma unwilling to accept another culture's view of the truth and so they *kill* each other over it. Also, on a less spectacular and more mundane level, we see relationships breaking up, marriages ending and co-workers bickering because of their differing views of what defines truth.

The God of Truth has the potential to be the most potent God in Waiting in your arsenal, but it requires you to have a *perspective* that the majority of the human race has yet to master. It requires you to understand that your truth is *exclusive* to you and has nothing *what so ever* to do with anyone else.

Throughout history there has been a great search for universal truth and when an individual or group thinks it has found it then the presumption is that *everyone* must accept it as *the* gospel truth. This is the main reason why there are wars. People mistakenly think that a truth needs to be accepted by the majority for it to be certified. Instead, what they're really showing, by their need for universal validation, is their *lack of belief* in that certain truth. I think Jesus wouldn't have opened up his mouth had he known what was going to be wrought in his name. He wanted people to find their own connection with god and *their own truth*. He certainly said nothing about churches, collection plates, robes, symbols and crusades. That's what he was *rejecting* when he went into the desert. He understood that truth is individual and he tried to pass that message along, but it was lost because it's *easier* to form groups than it is to blaze a trail as an individual.

When someone discovers a certain truth about the nature of reality it is certainly possible, even likely, others *will* agree with it and want to join with this truth. That is how religions, friendships, political parties and baseball teams are formed. But what is not understood is that *every person is different* and though he or she may accept your version of the truth, he or she is accepting it in *his or her* own way by either adding to it or subtracting from in order to make it fit his or her universe.

If we carry out this reasoning to its natural conclusion then no two people are the same and no single truth can ever apply to all. *And it's not supposed to!* What the God of Truth wants us to realize is that there are Five Billion plus people on this earth with five billion plus different and distinct truths. Some may be similar in parts, but no two can *ever* be the same.

The God of Truth wants you to find your own truth and he wants that truth to apply only to you. He forbids you to apply it anyone else. If, for example, the truth about yourself is that you hate everyone, then you are allowed to hate everyone, but that doesn't mean you can kill everyone because they don't see things like you do. The God of Truth says that *no one will ever see things exactly like you do so it pointless to kill someone because they don't?* They weren't *supposed* to in the first place! If fact, your truth should have *nothing* to do with anyone else. You will always be a religion of one.

Einstein said that the nature of reality is relative to the observer and such is the case when we look at the truth. It is and *has to be* relative to the observer. After all, who else is it relative too? I cannot get my truth from you and you cannot get it from me. It is one specific truth from one specific point of view in space and time.

Now, just because I consider everyone a religion of one and contend that we can never find another person who has the exact same truths as we do, it doesn't mean we can never connect with anyone. We connect with people all the time and form friendships and relationships with them. These people usually have *similar* truths to our own, but never exactly the same. They will and should be forever separate and on their own distinct road to actualization and awareness. And that's okay. That's the way the God of Truth wants it to be because the trouble begins when we want, need or force others to believe what we believe. It may sound funny, but if we all proceeded as if the views of other people in the world didn't matter then we *would all get along much better!* If we're truthful with ourselves, without taking anyone else into account, then we'll realize we are ultimately responsible for our own happiness or lack thereof and won't be upset when someone doesn't give it to us.

If you look at all of the notorious people throughout history you will see they were driven by an inability to deal with their own lives truthfully. The past and the present is littered with leaders like Hitler, who blamed an entire race for his and Germany's problems, or Osama Bin Laden who sees all of Western Culture as a threat to Islam and thus feels he has to wipe it out, or many of our Presidents who think that Democracy is a *just cause* that *must* spread for *the good of other people*. And they'll all make their points by *killing people* if necessary!

What these leaders show by their actions is really an *inability* to believe in their own truths. The Jewish race wasn't Hitler's problem; it was his own self-hatred and Germany's own self-loathing that created an atmosphere where hate could breed. If Bin Laden sees Western Culture with its low morals and materialism as a threat to Islamic Culture, then does he really think he's going to win the people of the world to his cause by killing people? And what is he saying about Islam as a religion and Muslim people as a whole if he feels they will succumb to the temptations of the West if given the chance? And the same can be said for President Bush's current philosophy. Is forcing Democracy on a country the way to extol the virtues of democracy? I don't think so.

What I'm really talking about here again is perspective. It's all just a matter of focusing your attention on *you* instead of on others. People may have wronged you, harmed you, but you can either blame them for the rest of your life or you can find a solution and take responsibility for your own happiness. Others may have contributed to your misery when you were child, but that doesn't mean you have let their sins follow you into adulthood. Doing that just means they still have control over your life, which just adds to your anger.

When you take responsibility for your happiness and believe in your own truth then you'll see something miraculous happen. You will find yourself taking responsibility for your life on and off the field, which, in turn, will give you more of an ability to communicate with the Gods of Control, Balance, Confidence and Self Esteem, as well as the Gods of Fear, Anger and Ego, which will help you play better baseball and live a better life.

I have found in my work as a coach, my days as a player, and my job as a Math Teacher that our biggest problem collectively is our inability to focus all the responsibility for our lack of success and happiness on ourselves. It is always someone else who needs to change *their truths* or to see something *they're not seeing*. On the field it's always the umpires fault or another teammate who blew the game. But even though our teammates can make blunders behind us, we are always in charge of how we *deal with it!* No one can ever put a dent in our truths unless we let them. If we believe there is meaning in life then there *is* meaning in life. If love is our truth then we must love *no matter what the situation.* Because, if we do, then we'll make it through the difficult circumstances and we'll help pull our teammates through as well...

Now, as a side note, there are situations in life where it *appears* on the surface that one must subjugate one's own truth to that of another. A player for example has a coach or a manager who calls all the shots. But, if one were to analyze this in terms of energy one would see that, although it appears as though the coach and the player may have truth issues that will make it impossible for them to coexist, they, in fact, don't. Each person has his role to perform and more importantly both have the same *objective*, which is to participate in the game of baseball and hopefully to perform well.

I have an example that I think illustrates what I just said in a way that makes it real...

I had a player once that I just couldn't get to listen to me. He had a pretty big chip on his shoulder and fought me every step of the way even at the expense of improving his talent, which if he had let me, I surely could have done. So one day I pulled him aside and said, "You don't like me much do you?"

At first he bite his lip and just shook his head yes even though his expression said no. So, I pressed him. I said, "C'mon, tell me the truth. I won't hold it against you."

He thought for a minute and summoned up enough courage and said, "No coach, I don't like you." And then he seemed to brace himself.

When I heard him speak his mind I felt relieved because I knew that from that moment on things were going to get better. And why did I think that? I thought it because the truth was being told and the truth, if you're strong enough to say it, and brave enough to ask for it really does set you free.

After he spoke, he just stood there staring at me like a deer in the headlights. I'm sure he was expecting the hammer to fall. But instead, I looked him in the eye and said right back to him, "You know what? I don't like you much either," which surprised him. But I didn't stop there. I explained further because I knew that the magic of truth had given me a window of opportunity to solve the problem. I continued on and said: "It's okay that you don't like me and it's okay that I don't care for you; we aren't going to like every single person we meet in our lives. But, now that we have laid our cards on the table, that doesn't mean we can't do what we came here together to do, which is for me to teach you how to play better, which you know I can do, and for you to play better, which you know you can do, and ultimately for us to win games, which I know we both want to do. I understand you don't like my style of coaching, but you have to understand that I am just being me, just like you are just being you. But what we do have in common is that we *both* love baseball. So let's just concentrate on each one of us doing our *jobs* and see where it takes us."

After I finished talking, there was a moment of silence. I could almost hear him thinking to himself, *is he bullshitting me? Is he bullshitting me?* Then slowly, as if the wall was coming down brick by brick, a look of relief came over his face and he looked at me straight on and said, "I can do that." Then he turned and walked away and I could almost see the weight being lifted off his shoulders. I had been truthful with him and more importantly I had *allowed* him to be truthful with me, which I think is all he really wanted.

Two years later during his senior season I would often hear him yelling at kids during practice because they were complaining about me being tough on them. Once I overheard him say, "Hey you might not like coach but at least he's straight with you and you have to respect that even if you don't like it. If you've got a problem then be a man and say it to him."

When our final season together ended, he came into my office for the last time and we shook each other's hand and gave each other a look of recognition. We were still two warriors who had different ways of looking at things, but we put it aside because *it didn't really matter.* My truth was mine and his was his, but that didn't mean they couldn't coexist and accomplish great things together. In the end, whether or not we wanted to admit it, our truths did bring us closer together because that's what truths do, if you're open to seeing the truth about yourself. And that is the key.

Of course there will be times when things won't ever reach the point of being ideal. Sometimes it's just impossible for people to accept each other's truths, and that's okay. We don't have to like each other. We don't even have to respect each other. But we do have to *tolerate* each other because the nature of truth tells us that we have to. If there can never be a universal truth for all people at all times then we must realize that *everyone* is different from us and accept *that* as the truth.

THE GOD OF EXERCISE

After discussing the complexities and the passions evoked by the God of Truth, it will be nice to take look at a god, like the God of Exercise, who is simple and straightforward, yet powerful in its own right.

Everybody knows what exercise is whether one plays baseball or not. But not many really know *why* exercise is important beyond the obvious improved physical capabilities it gives us. Exercise is not just a way to increase our speed or muscle strength, and it's not just something we use to help us lose weight or to make us look good on the beach. The God of Exercise is not interested in merely in making our bodies into machines capable of hitting baseballs farther or throwing them faster; it has loftier goals to attain.

When we exercise we can focus on the act of what we're doing from two distinct and different points of view. We can observe it from an egotistical point of view or from an enlighten perspective as a means to achieve more body awareness.

If we chose to look at exercise from an egotistical point of view we see ourselves with an inflated image with every mile we run or weight we lift. We feel intoxicated with the raw power of our bodies as they perform. Just take a peek inside a gym or a health club someday and you'll see what I mean. There is a glow of self-importance around many as they sculpt their bodies for future performances on the field, on the beach or in the bedroom. But if you do chose this path then you will be open to all the pain the God of Ego can inflict on you.

The second point of view we can choose is to look at exercise as a means by which we can increase awareness of ourselves both physically and spiritually. There is nothing an athlete needs more than body awareness and exercise is the best way to achieve that state. The act of exercising forces us to get in touch with the muscles in our body as we push them to their limit during exercise. We can feel our quads burn as we run up a hill, our pecks tighten as we squeeze out one last rep and our diaphragms howl as our lungs try to expand beyond their limit in an attempt to gather every bit of oxygen they can to keep us going. The God of Exercise wants us to *feel* these things because when we do they connect the spirit with the body.

It is essential to be able to feel every muscle in the body and to know what it is capable of doing if we are ever to become a top-notch athlete. When we swing and connect for a line drive base hit we need to *feel* what it takes to accomplish that act. We need to be aware of what our muscles are doing at the time, and where the parts of our body are positioned so we can know how to duplicate these feelings every time we are at the plate. This is why so many athletes look at film when they are in slumps. It's because they're trying to *see* what their bodies were doing when they were performing these acts *correctly* and they hope they can translate what they see on film and apply it to their current slump. But, as I hope I've shown in this book, the answer doesn't come from looking at film, it comes from looking at yourself and figuring out why you have lost touch with yourself and your body. The reason is rarely physical unless there is an injury causing the problem. It is instead your inability to understand what the Gods are trying to tell you about yourself. Sure looking at film helps a little in that it will help you *see* what you were doing correctly in the past, but if you remain the same person then you will continue to make the same mistakes and never get to the *feeling* of doing things right.

When I played college ball in the northeast at Southern Connecticut State University, it was so cold in the spring we were always at a disadvantage when it came to getting ourselves ready for the up coming season. We would have to practice inside and do most of our pitching and hitting in cages and in makeshift indoor fields. But there was one coach, Frank "Porky" Viera at the University of New Haven, who took a radically different approach that yielded him awesome results and fitted nicely with what I believe is the role of the God of Exercise in sports.

What Coach Viera used to do at the beginning of every season was to spend the first three weeks just exercising…and exercising…and exercising without *ever* picking up a baseball or a bat. His workouts were grueling and legendary. There wasn't a team in the Northeast that hadn't heard of the regime his players went through. He made his players pray to the God of Exercise and the effects were magical.

When Coach V. made his players go through his "ritual" of extreme physical exertion, it toughened them up and forced them to look within for the strength they needed to make it through. It also made them look to each other for support, which created a camaraderie and closeness that one can only call a "team". The experience *bonded* them. What he did with this method was to construct a well of energy so deep and powerful that the opposing team could feel it the minute his team started to go through their pre-game warm-ups. In most cases the game was over right there during batting practice. Because of the powerful energy they exuded we would see them as unbeatable and so consequently they were.

During the 60's, 70's, 80's and 90's, the University of New Haven would make the Division II College World Series with regularity, where they would compete and defeat many of the warm weather teams. Coach V's methods made good players great and average players good and that is what the Gods can do when they are tapped into. To this day Coach Viera has over 1000 wins and is considered legendary in the world of College Baseball…

There is no position on the field where body awareness comes into play more than it does for the pitcher. He must, on a continual basis, monitor his body in order to stay in balance and keep his arm in its slot. Every pitch is a testament to his ability to stay in touch with his motion and with the Gods because every little change in energy can throw him off. A pitcher, unlike batters who have time between at bats to connect with their energy, must do it from pitch to pitch over the course of the entire game. He must not only be able to throw the ball over the plate, he must also be able throw it to different *parts* of the plate and at different speeds. All this requires a continuous updating of self-awareness and communication with the body because you never know when a God may show up, say right before the biggest pitch of the game, and challenge you to make the right pitch. There's nothing like being 3-2 on a batter with the bases loaded and two outs in the last inning of tie game and having the God of Fear pop up to see if you have the courage to make the pitch you need to make. But being aware of your body through the God of Exercise gives you a wellspring of energy and awareness, which you can tap into to help you overcome the God of Fear. And again, the awareness I'm talking about is not the kind that has the playing "thinking" he must put his arm here and his leg there. It is the kind that has him in the flow and *feeling* what is right for his body.

I get a kick when I'm jogging down the street and I see people running or biking by me and they have headphones on listening to music. Or when I hear people say to me that running is "boring" and they can't do it. I think to myself, *you don't know what you're missing!* When I jog there is so much going on inside me that I hardly know the time is passing. I run for an hour at a time and I'm sad when the run is over because there was so much left to experience both internally and externally.

I can understand why a person would want to escape himself. The truth is not easy to face. It is much easier to find things to distract us from facing ourselves. But the fact remains that no matter how well we *think* we are distracting ourselves or hiding from the reality of our lives, we can never escape the pure relentless power of the soul's need to be heard. And the God of Exercise is a great way for your soul to express itself…So the next time you exercise, instead of focusing on your ego or looking for ways to distract yourself so the time will go by faster, focus your energy on what your body is feeling and trying to tell you. You won't be sorry…

Post Game Wrap-Up

Throughout the book I have categorized the Baseball Gods as "Major", "Minor" and the "Gods in Waiting". All of these Gods play a critical role in the shaping of the athlete as a ballplayer and more importantly as a person. They communicate, to those who want to listen, messages of the past, present and future. They expose us to the core of who we really are.

When a pitcher a goes through his wind up—a batter attempts to hit a pitched ball—a fielder positions himself to make a play or a manager ponders a decision, the Gods arrive to give us a snap shot of where we are at the present moment in our evolution as a human being. Using myself as an example, as I've done throughout most of this book, I can look back at the arc of my life and see where I've grown as both a player and a person. When I was a kid playing in Little League I had no control of my pitches and used to walk the ballpark. I would live in fear of being in a situation where I might fail and thus diminish my already decimated self-esteem. I would live my life on an emotional roller coaster teetering back and forth between a love for the game and a hatred for the albatross it was becoming in my life. Fast forward thirty years later and I'm a pitcher who rarely walks a batter, has his emotions fairly balanced and under control and who is less and less a victim of his own ignorance and low self esteem. And even when I do fall victim to my own shortcomings, I know where to look for the answers. I look to myself and I listen to the Gods…

But the story doesn't end here because I have purposely left out one essential God, although; I have alluded to it throughout this book. You may have figured it out by now or maybe you haven't. It's a God who *must* be part of the equation if we are to have any chance at all of hearing and deciphering any of their lessons. It is the God that came *before* all the other gods…

The God of Love

There is something or someone in everyone's life that they love more than anything, even themselves. It may not be something that puts them in the spotlight, like playing the national pastime, but that doesn't matter because love isn't the sole property of the famous athlete. Instead, love resides in the domain of the heart of anyone who has ever given his or her soul over to something completely. It's not what you *do* that matters it's whether or not you have given your life over to it that does. Only when you love something more than you love yourself can you hear the whispers of the Gods and begin to learn what they have to teach you.

When a person loves something more than himself, like baseball for example, it opens him up to the Gods. It puts him in a state of *vulnerability* that the Gods seize upon to make their points. They don't do this because they want to ruin his good time, but because they know his love makes him *want to learn more* about the game and himself, otherwise he wouldn't love it; he would only love himself instead.

Of course, many people do things in life they don't love and they do these things for various reasons all of which block the efforts of the Gods to enlighten. Besides the Ego, which I've already discussed in length, people do things for other ego-related reasons. These reasons include things like money and security, which allow them to "fit into" society so they can take the path of least resistance. It is this path of least resistance that has turned western culture from one that was vital and in touch with the Gods to one that is now an empty gilded cage, a Black Hole that can't seem to consume enough substance to fill up the void that resides within...

The God of Love is a well-worn, misunderstood and misused God. Many people *say* they love something, but precious few really *mean* what they say or *back it up* with deeds. That being said, what does it mean to truly love something or someone? What does it mean when we say, "I love you" or "I love to play baseball"? We hear these words said all the time and we have used them ourselves, but what do they really *mean*?

Every culture throughout the history of human civilization has expressed what it means to love. You can see it in their religious ceremonies, in their art and in their philosophies. Love has certainly been everywhere century after century, expressed beautifully in plays, poems and song, but actual love between two people or races or countries still seems to be in short supply. The question is why?

We have all heard the saying that "you have to love yourself before you can love someone else". The reason why this saying has gotten so much attention is because it has become apparent that people look to others to give them what they lack in life and this has caused heartache and despair because no one can give you what you lack in your life, only you can. But, even though you can't rely on people to "make you happy", the one thing that is worrisome about this statement is that it is *dysfunctional* to love yourself. If you love yourself then you are falling prey to the God of Ego. You can only love *something* or *someone* or *be loved* by someone. The key to feeling love inside you is not to love yourself, but to love something else *other* than yourself totally and completely...

The problem with love throughout history is that people have used it in order to get something back. When someone says, "I love you" they hope to hear it in return, but this is not love, not according to the God of Love. If you love the game of baseball because you are good at it and it brings you success or money or ego gratification or self esteem then you don't really love it. You are *using it* to fulfill *your* needs and desires and not anything else. Love does not use anything for its own gratification. Love is *selfless*. That is the only way it can be.

When I was younger I played baseball because I *wanted* things from it. Yes, I dedicated my life to it, which was noble, but I needed it to validate *me*. That's why, after college, when I didn't get drafted to play pro ball; I gave the game up. It could no longer give me anything.

Now, at forty-two years old and with nothing to be gained, I play the game because I love it and that's why I am finally able to hear what the Gods have been trying to tell me my whole life. There are no fans at our games, no newspaper articles to be cut out and pasted in a scrape book and certainly no money ever to be made. There are only sore muscles, ever degenerating ability and painful memories of what could have been juxtaposed to the crack of the bat, pop of the mitt after an occasional good fastball and the friendships made with men like myself who long to feel innocent again. That is what love is. It isn't flashy and full of pomp and circumstance. It is serene and pure and understated like a trail that weaves through the woods and goes nowhere in particular, but that somehow makes you feel good after walking it.

When we do anything in life like play baseball or have relationships we must do so without expectations and without resistance. We must play baseball as if we were worshipping God. We must do this not because of what Baseball can do for us, but because of what *we could do for it!* We must make ourselves vulnerable because if we are only thinking about our needs and wants then we become myopic and closed off to the world around us without a chance of seeing or hearing the Gods…

When I was a kid I lived and breathed the music of the Beatles and one of the songs I played over and over was "All You Need Is Love". It was a song that defined the Sixties and the "Summer of Love" of 1967, but like the entire "Flower Power" movement it never really showed or explained what you were supposed *to do* in order to get the love you need. I guess that's what I'm trying to do here. John Lennon was 100% correct when he sang those words. Love is really all you need and I hope I've given you some insight here in this book what it feels like to have it and what it takes to get it!

Questions and Answers

At the end of every professional game, the media descends on the locker room to ask a litany of mundane questions, which then leads to a litany of cliché answers from the players and coaches. We've heard it all before. Players stand there and talk about how great they feel about hitting the game winning homerun and winning the World Championship or worse they thank *God* or *Jesus* for helping them win as if Jesus cared only about helping the *winning team!* But rarely if ever do I hear players become humble before the game and frame their win in a perspective of wisdom and humility. Precious few times have I heard a player talk about how lucky and blessed he is to be playing a kid's game for living or how he owed it all to his father or his mother or his teammates. But when I do hear a sincere answer, an answer that sees the big picture, I smile because I know that player "gets it". He understands the Gods. He knows that life has meaning...

And so now, as the Baseball Gods head to the locker room, I promise I will not subject them to a bunch of mundane questions. I will not reduce them to the banality that we so often hear after the game is over and I can also guarantee you that their answers will not be laden with clichés.

I've come upon these questions in a variety of ways. Some have imposed their will during games I've either played in or coached, but most have come off the field while jogging in the silence of the woods or in my backyard where I've spent the better part of the last thirty years practicing my pitching by throwing against an old mattress...

How do I contact the Gods?

Every culture has its way of contacting its God or Gods. The followers of today's major religions go to some type of church, mosque or temple and pray in an attempt to gain an audience with the divine. They perform rituals laid down over thousands of years, which they hope will *connect* them to the original inspiration. Other Pagan Religions, like our own Native American, also perform rituals with the same goal in mind. They seek an audience with the divine.

There really is no difference in religions when they are broken down into their basic building blocks. They all involve a ritual or rituals, inspired by an enlightened prophet, that if adhered to will *shatter* the illusion of this "real world" we experience with our five senses and *transport* us to a state of transcendence that a holy man would call the "real" nature of reality. We've all heard of these methods of transportation. The Buddhists meditate, the Christians pray, the Zen Monks practice strict repetition of ritual acts such as archery, the Native Americans go on Vision Quests and Baseball Players like me play the game they love all in an attempt to seek an audience with the divine.

The Baseball Gods, like any other Gods, reside in various types of cathedrals which we call baseball fields, parks, stadiums, sandlots, backyards or any patch of earth where kids or adults gather to perform the ritual we call the game of baseball. But unlike the members of religions who have to seek out their God through prayer, ball players just have to show up at the field and wait for the Baseball Gods to come to *them!*

The Baseball Gods are pro-active. They don't wait for people to have an epiphany so they can find religion. They are right there in your face like a drill sergeant during basic training constantly probing your soul for weaknesses that need to be attended to if you are ever to become whole. So don't worry about whether or not the Baseball Gods will listen to you when you pray. What you should be focusing on is whether or not you will be listening to *them* when they are trying to get your attention.

IS THERE SUCH A THING AS THE CURSE OF THE BAMBINO?

As I am writing this book I'm watching the Yankees play the Red Sox in the 2004 League Championship Series and the Yankees are up three games to none and about to sweep the Red Sox...It's been a interesting coincidence writing about the Gods and the Curse as I'm watching it unfold in front of my eyes...

Of course, here in Northeast where I live, all I've heard about for the past week is the "Curse of the Bambino". If one listens to Sports Talk Radio one will hear fans talk of "the curse", but most analysts dismiss it as a creation of the media and people's fertile imagination. Oh sure, they may use it to liven up their shows, but no one really *believes* in it. But then again why should they? There is no precedence in western culture that says such things, as curses, are real. Western culture believes in science and substance and things that can be proved and measured empirically. But as I've already explained, reality has nothing to do with substance. It has to do with energy, pure energy. That's all there is to reality and the "Curse" is most definitely pure energy that has taken the *form* of the Red Sox not winning the World Series since 1918, and that's why it is as real as the field they play on!

The energy of the "Curse of the Bambino" is as potent as any in sports and I believe it comes directly from the Red Sox Nation. It is lodged deep within the psyche of fans that *expect* something to go wrong, which is then passed on to the players. It is the fans *collective energy*, which creates the result. After 86 years of futility, it is burned so deeply into the collective unconscious of the fans and players that they don't *know* any other way. Like a family heirloom, it keeps on getting passed down from generation to generation. Whereas, on the contrary, the Yankees fans *expect* something *good* to happen and their organization *expects* to win. That is really what is at the heart of the curse. It is *belief*. It isn't material. It is energy.

I think it's fair for me to say that most of the players on the Red Sox have been winners at some points in their careers or else they would have never made it as far as the Major Leagues. I'm sure if you checked there have been numerous Little League, Babe Ruth, American Legion, High School State Championships, Collegiate and Minor League titles spread among the Red Sox players. These players, like the players from the Red Sox past, haven't always been losers of the "big game" yet they come up short year after year, and it is because of the overpowering expectation of failure from the fans and the media that has strangled the players' ability to perform well. It has *infected* them and let the God of Fear seep into the field of play.

Now, in order for me to make an assertion like this, I'm going to need to offer up some kind of proof. The first thing I'm going to do is to look at some specific high profile players. In 1977 Mike Torres was a critical part of the Yankees pitching staff when they won the World Series over the Dodgers. The next year he was the goat for the Red Sox after he gave up the famous Bucky Dent Homerun in the 1978 one game playoff for the division. And then there was Wade Boggs who spent most of his career in Boston on the losing end in the playoffs until he came to the Yankees where he drew a key walk to help the Yankees win the World Series. And lastly, there was Roger Clemens who, although one of the most dominant pitchers in the history of baseball, never could quite come up with the dominant performance in the playoffs *until* he came to the Yankees.

Wait, what's this...I'm watching the ninth inning of game four with the Sox down by a run and about to get swept...but something is happening...

Cut to: Game Four Ninth Inning, Fenway Park, Yankees up 4 to 3 with the great Mariano Rivera on the mound for the Yankees.

The Red Sox start off the inning with a walk, then a stolen base and then a base hit. Game tied. Fans go berserk. Red Sox win in extra innings. Games five and six also go the Red Sox! Game five was ANOTHER come from behind win! And game six was never in doubt. This group of Red Sox is staring the curse down. Will it blink?

Cut to: Game Seven.

I can't believe what I'm seeing. The Red Sox are hammering the Yankees at Yankee Stadium. There are 56,000 people there and it sounds like morgue. Everything Joe Torre tries is akin to pouring gas on the fire. The Red Sox are actually going to beat the Yankees. I can't believe it. Can you tell I'm a Yankees fan? But of course, this doesn't mean the Red Sox will win the World Series. The Curse is still hanging around out there like a vulture about to pick on the remains of the carcass...

Cut: Game four of the World Series against the St Louis Cardinals.

It's like the Red Sox are playing against some Little League Team. The Sox are just punishing the Cardinals for the fourth game in a row. The Red Sox are finally going to win the World Series after 86 years! It's like the polarity of the earth has suddenly shifted. Is this the end of the world?

What the hell just happened? Let's take a look at it...

Despite eighty-six years of negative energy, the Red Sox have finally won the World Series. The question is how did they do it? Well, according to the Baseball Gods, the Red Sox players collectively were able to summon up enough energy and belief in themselves to overcome the entire amount of negative sent their way. And, without knowing it, I believe the very same media that had fostered the "Curse" for so many years actually helped them along.

The Red Sox, throughout the span of this curse, have had the uncanny ability to snatch defeat from the jaws of victory, but in the 2004 ALCS against the Yankees they finally snatched victory from the jaws of defeat. Trailing 4-3 in the 9th and down three games to zero, with the greatest reliever in the history of the post season on the mound for the Yankees, Mariano Rivera, the Sox miraculously came back to win the game, which injected a positive energy into the team that had never been there in the 86 years prior. They went on from that moment to do something that had never been done in baseball history, which was to come back and win a series after being down three games to zero. So the question is: "What happened?" And how did the media help the Red Sox come back to win?

When the Red Sox beat the Yankees, after being down three games to none, the things that were repeated over and over by the media were how much the guys *loved* each other and how much *fun* they were having playing together. They said there was an *obvious positive energy* pulsating through the team that bound twenty-five individual baseball players into one. But that praise by the media was *post hoc*. It happened *after* the Red Sox had beaten the Yankees. The media was trying to jump on the bandwagon, but it was too late. The Red Sox as a team didn't need them or their fans anymore because they had already ascended to Pantheon of the Gods by their belief in each other.

Twenty-five baseball players bound as one is certainly a force to be reckoned with and I believe this alone was enough to overcome 86 years of the "Curse of the Bambino", but something else also happened to seal the deal. As the Yankees and the Red Sox were preparing to play game seven of their series, I was listening to a twenty-four hour sports radio station in New York called WFAN and I heard one of their hosts say something that I believe was right on the mark in relation to "the curse".

The host speculated that, because the Red Sox's media and fans had pronounced them dead after game three, they had turned them into ghosts and who better to battle the ghosts of their past than another ghost! Well, after this host shared his little theory, his co-host laughed, as I'm sure most of the listeners did, at what a creative thought it was, but then little else was said about it. But what could they say? Western culture has always given a short rift to curses and things that reek of the occult. This is, after all, a scientific culture and ideas must be empirically verified if they are to hold any weight. But if you were talking to a Native American or an Ancient Greek well…it might have be a different story…

There is one last point of significance that I noticed during the Red Sox miraculous run to the World Series Championship. After they completed their historic comeback against the Yankees, they moved on to the World Series against the St. Louis Cardinals and throughout the series the Red Sox faithful, buoyed by the victory over the Yankees held up signs that said, "believe".

Now, when people say, "believe" everyone seems to know what it means. But what does it mean? What exactly is belief? Can you point to something and say: "That is belief over there"? Or can you go to a store and ask the clerk for a pound of belief? The answer is no, you can't.

Belief is something that doesn't exist, but yet it exists. It is something that we understand completely, but yet have no clue what it is. It is not empirically verifiable and certainly not scientific and so we get no help from the scientific community to define it for us. In fact, according to science, belief *doesn't even exist!* But belief, like the Baseball Gods, is just as real as the bats, balls and gloves we use to play the game. We see evidence of it all around us on the Baseball Field and, if we're paying attention, in our everyday lives as well. *Our beliefs and our energy really do create our reality* and that is what made the Red Sox win the World Series. And nothing else…

WHY DO SOME PLAYERS ALWAYS GET INJURED WHILE OTHERS DON'T?

Have you ever wondered why some players are constantly injured while others never seem to get bitten by the injury bug? It's something I've wondered about for years and to this day I've rarely heard any professional attempt to answer the question. It is usually just attributed to bad luck or even worse to some catch all phrase like, "well he's just an injury prone player", like that that is supposed to answer the question! Or they point to physical defects in his body that are causing the constant injuries. The Gods have quite a bit to say about injuries and the injury prone player. Let's take a look at this mysterious subject...

Every now and then you hear about studies that makes the connection between stress and disease or injury. The maladies studied range from Cancer to Migraine Headaches to Back Problems to High Blood Pressure, but doctors, like scientist, ignore the possibility of stress (energy) as the *main factor*, because it is hard to gather data about it, and so they usually go on to suggest some type of drug to "cure" the illness. Sometimes they mention using meditation or yoga, as a means of relaxation, but that is usually a periphery solution. The emphasis is almost always centered on a biological treatment with drugs or operations. But then why should it be any other way? To our scientific culture anything less would look like voodoo medicine and should be saved for the National Geographic Channel, but kept out of the doctor's office. But there *are* fields of study in the therapeutic world that deal with the relationship between the physical body and energy. We've all heard of Acupuncture, Reflexology and Aroma Therapy, but the field I'm going to discuss is relatively unknown one called Somatic Therapy. It is an approach born from the womb of the Gods.

The theory behind the Somatic approach is that the energy generated by our feelings and emotions is stored within certain muscles. For example, if you are the type that feels the weight of the world is on your shoulders then it will store itself in the shoulders and back. If you have been abused in any way as a child then you'll store that feeling of fear in the muscles that tightened in anticipation of the abuse.

When looking at our "injury prone" player from a Somatic perspective we see the injuries popping up to put on face on issues that the person needs to work out. Once a player has been stopped by an injury it gives him the opportunity to stop, look and listen to what is going on in his life. The injury does, in effect, exactly what the Gods want it to do, which is to focus the player on himself.

There are a few books on the market that connect certain feelings with particular body parts. My favorite book is "Heal Your Body" by Louis Hay. It is an encyclopedia of the connection between your spiritual energy and your physical body and I've used it many times to enlighten me when I've been consumed by physical ailments. There are also numerous websites on Somatic Therapy that explain how it attempts to release the stored up negative energy thereby creating a more *balanced* and healthy body.

As with every other concept I've discussed in this book, the key is that you proceed on the belief that life is meaningful. If life *is* meaningful then *injuries* are also meaningful and not just a physical nuisance caused by some freak accident that just needs time to heal. Instead, they are spiritual lessons given to you in order for you to learn. Everything happens for a reason…everything. It can be no other way or else life has no meaning at all.

All of the Major and Minor Gods can manifest their energy through injuries in the body. I've covered many of the ways these Gods affect our feelings, but as I've shown these feelings do manifest themselves into a physical reality on the field in the form of hits, runs and errors. They can also manifest themselves as physical injuries as well. It all depends on what the Gods feel is the best way to get our attention.

If a player is in the grips of the God of Fear his body will be saddled with that negative energy as it tries to perform. If he's a pitcher he may grip the ball too tight or try to throw it too hard, which will result in elbow, back or shoulder problems. If he's a batter, say a young batter, who is afraid of getting hit with the pitched ball then, sure as the sun will come up tomorrow, he will get plunked and hurt by a pitch.

There is a saying in baseball that the "ball will always find you". What this means is that what you fear most will be *drawn* to you. If you're afraid of making an error in the field then you can bet the next ground ball will be hit right at you. If you're a coach trying to hide a weak player somewhere in the field then you can be certain a ball will find him, and at the worst possible time. *Feelings manifest themselves as reality.*

A few years back, one of my pitchers from the High School team I coached had a break out year as a sophomore. He led us to the State Class L Finals and received a great deal of press and attention from pro and college scouts. The next season he came in highly touted, with great expectations, and I could tell right away he wasn't handling the change too well. He was comfortable with the role of unknown underdog. But, as the spotlight began to shine on him, I could see him begin to crumble. Soon the injuries began to pop up.

It was about a week into our spring training when he came to me and said his elbow was sore. I told him to ice it and take a couple of days off. I knew there was no way he could possibly have tendonitis in his elbow, but I went along with it. It had to be the pressure of the lofty expectations placed on him by his family, friends and by me.

After a couple days off, I had him throw and once again he complained of pain in his elbow. So, for the second time, I told him to ice it, take some Advil and rest it for a couple of days. I knew I was dealing with more than just physical pain, but I wasn't sure what to do. The Gods were calling and I needed answers, quick.

My pitcher's elbow problems continued unabated for another two weeks until there were only a handful of days left before the start of the season. I tried to help him to see that his pain was really just his fears manifesting themselves in his elbow, but I couldn't get anywhere with him. It's tough for anyone to ignore the hard reality of pain, because when faced with a choice between a spiritual explanation and a physical explanation, the physical will always win out in our culture. It has to...no other precedent has been set.

With only a few days left before the start of our season, I decided to roll the dice. My plan was to shock him into breaking free from the God of Fear. I wanted to, in a sense, *really give him something to be afraid of!* So I went up to him, after a practice that saw him debilitated again, and told him I was going to talk to his parents about "shutting him down" for the season...

I said the words to him in a matter of fact tone that was devoid of the empathy I had been showing him earlier. I knew he needed strength and strength was what I was going to show him. I had babied him through his crisis long enough and now it was time to tune him into reality.

It was a mere seconds after I finished telling him he was through for the season that *real fear* began to wash over him like a cold hard rain. He protested immediately and wanted to know "why?" So I looked at him straight in the eye and told him that something must *"really be wrong with his elbow"* for him to be unable to practice for two weeks and that I wasn't going to see him permanently damage himself and his future.

Now, at this point, I knew my gamble could go one of two ways. My pitcher could use this as the excuse he needed to avoid all the pressures and expectations or he could face the *"real fear"* of not being able to play and thus overcome the pain.

The next day at practice I watched as the guys came strolling into the locker room and soon my star pitcher came in with a big smile on his face looking like the weight of the world had been lifted from his shoulders. He came over to me as I was pulling out the equipment and said: "Coach, I iced my arm and took a bunch of Advil last night and I feel fine today". "I don't feel any pain", he said, as he mimicked the throwing motion. "I feel great". And that was that. I never heard another word about his sore elbow for the rest of the spring and he went on to have a good season and is currently pitching well in college.

Now, I'm not going to say here that all injuries can be rectified so easily or that they all can be healed with a spiritual solution. Sometimes the spirit has been ignored for so long that the physical is permanently damaged. But I am saying that their root cause is not in our bodies, but in our spirit. And if the roots can be understood and dealt with then the effects can be healed…

At this point I think it's also important to say that biological solutions, meaning medicinal drugs or operations to physical problems, do have validity. The reason for this is that drugs and operations have energies of their *own* and do have the capability to change the energy of a person. But the problem with biological solutions is that, if the *feeling* that caused the problem in the first place has yet to be addressed, no lasting change will ever really take place.

When a person gets to the point of a biological solution this means the Gods have been ignored for so long that his own energy has been usurped. The insertion of a biological solution can help to replace the body's lost energy and give him another opportunity to face the Gods, but face the Gods he must or he will be battling the same physical problems over and over again.

In the perfect world of the Baseball Gods there would be no need for medicine or operations of any type, but we are just mere mortals trying to cope and so we must do what can to survive because "where there is life there is hope".

WHAT DO THE GODS HAVE TO SAY ABOUT THE YIPS?

Every now and then a player comes along that, for some unknown reason, has a complete meltdown and can no longer perform the simple baseball skills that he once had mastered. When I was a kid and infatuated with the 1971 Pirates, I watched in amazement as my favorite pitcher Steve Blass suddenly could no longer throw the ball anywhere near the strike zone. He went from a World Series hero in 71', 19-8 in 72', to oblivion in 1973. Just like that! He simply couldn't throw the ball over the plate anymore. (In retrospect I think it's interesting that *he* was my favorite pitcher!) Next was Steve Sax, the flashy second basemen for the Dodgers who, in the 80's, fought the yips while throwing the ball from second to first. Then, also in the 80's, was Mets' catcher Mackey Sasser whose career was shortened because he couldn't throw the ball back to the pitcher! And lastly, in the 90's, there were former Yankees' second baseman Chuck Knoblauch, and Cardinals' young pitching star Rick Ankiel, both of whom could no longer control where they were throwing the ball. Knoblauch, a Gold Glover with the nickname "Fundamentally Sound Chuck Knoblauch" had to move to the outfield and then out of baseball because of his inability to correct his throwing problem. And, as I write this book, Ankiel is *still* trying to make his way back to the majors five years after melting down during a playoff game that saw him go from rookie phenom to freak show.

What happened to these players? How did they go from superstars to humorous anecdotes? These questions are legitimate and haunting and deserve answers, but few have been forth coming in the years since their demise. (Although it should be noted that Steve Sax did have success in overcoming his throwing issues)

When trying to find solutions for "the yips" most people tend to look at what is physically wrong first and then try to make adjustments from that perspective. They analyze the throwing motion and look for correctable flaws much in the same way a pitcher or hitter does when he is in a slump. But, as I've already shown, the answers will not be found in looking exclusively at the physical causes because, if you don't change the renegade energy that has thrown off the mechanics, then each physical adjustment will do nothing more then move the problem to a new area.

After the player with the yips looks for and exhausts all the possible physical solutions, one begins to hear the press start to talk about the possible *psychological* causes for the problem. The media then starts to dig into the *personal life* of the individual for the deep dark secrets that might be at the core of his demise. We often hear about marital troubles or childhood trauma as reasons for the mysterious yips. And though the media does this because they just want to make the story juicier, they are in effect *getting closer* to the actual cause of the problem.

When a player with the yips gets to the point of looking at psychological issues as causes for his problem he is getting *closer to the solution* because he's moved away from the physical, but he has stopped at the mind/brain instead of the spirit. The problem is not in the "mind". The mind/brain could care less about the yips. It has a body to run. The problem is with the player's feelings and the spiritual energy they control. It is that spiritual energy which affects the brain's ability to work efficiently and ultimately causes the physical body to malfunction. For example, when a child is fed a diet rich in fear you can bet he will be afraid. When a child is fed a diet dominated by hatred it is likely he will grow up with this energy inside him. How it will manifest itself and the *extent* of its manifestation will be different for every person but it *will* manifest itself. But for our purposes, as lovers of baseball, it will manifest itself on the field and this is where we can learn from it.

As with every God I've discussed so far, there has been some energy that has affected the player's ability to perform. And, with every discussion, I've also talked about things that can be done to change that energy. The yips are an energy that can be changed, but unlike the other gods I've discussed, the yips affect the person in a much more debilitating way because they *take away* the player's ability to play the game even though the person is physically capable! And this is doubly tough. If a pitcher can't throw the ball anywhere near the plate, he is not going to be allowed to pitch, plain and simple. Likewise, if a second baseman can't throw the ball to first, he can't play second base. He is stopped cold.

The player that has been affected by the yips is one who has a powerful energy inside him that needs to be dealt with and something within the sport he is playing has activated it. It has become the perfect marriage between the spiritual and the physical where the physical reality helps to release the imprisoned energy, much in the way vigorous massages, Yoga or Somatic Therapy release feelings from deep within our painful childhood experiences.

In the case of the yips, the player must remove himself from the game so he can gain perspective because it is impossible to gain perspective while in the middle of the hurricane. The yips are telling him that his problems are *bigger* than the game. The yips have over ridden his ability to play and that makes them a powerful force. And powerful forces must be dealt with or they become even more destructive forces. It may be brave to deal with them head on while still actively playing, but it is playing with fire. The Gods, by stopping us cold, are telling us that our life outside the game must take precedence. And as always, we must listen to the Gods.

The player with the yips may come back to the game someday or he may not. It just depends on the issues at hand. Some issues may take the rest of a person's life to deal with. I do think it's important to try to get back to the game because that's where the problem came to the surface, but, in the end, it is one's happiness and peace of mind that is the ultimate game we are playing. Maybe the yips are telling us in their own special way that we are meant to do other things. Maybe playing baseball was our way of fulfilling some else's dream and not an expression of our own spirit. It just depends on the person. The reasons are infinite and only the individual will ever really know...

HOW DO THE GODS FEEL ABOUT STEROIDS?

The issues surrounding steroids are of concern to the Gods, but not for the same reasons they are to Major League Baseball or to the members of Congress who are investigating their use. The Commissioner of Baseball and the Representatives of Congress are interested because steroids are illegal drugs and their use is against the laws of the land. They are also concerned because the *integrity* of the game is compromised by their use. The players using the drugs have an obvious energy advantage over their counterparts and are, in effect, cheating because their team has a better chance at winning the game.

The Baseball Gods are also interested in the use of steroids, but not because they affect the outcome of the game; they could care less about that. The Gods care because steroids are flares, warning signs, which help expose and draw attention to the problems of their users. Remember the Gods are concerned about the game of life not just the game. Their aim is to enlighten not to win the World Series.

The steroid user has in a sense gone over to the dark side. He is either so wrapped up in his ego or in the grips of fear and anger that he feels he must do whatever it takes to protect his false image of himself. The player who uses steroids is in deep trouble. His worship of the God of Ego has turned to fanaticism. He is so afraid of people seeing him as weak that he has decided to break the laws of both heaven and earth.

What the steroid user must do is to accept the fact that he and his issues have been exposed. He must come clean about his use, not because the fans and the league want him to, but because it is the *hardest thing to do*. It is *humiliating* and *humbling* and is the antidote he needs to rid himself of the God of Ego. He can't worry about what others may think of him because it isn't their place to judge him. His only responsibility is to the Gods. He answers to them and only them.

IS THERE A DIFFERENCE BETWEEN FEELINGS AND EMOTIONS?

If you listen to athletes, coaches or announcers, you'll often hear them talking about feelings and emotions as if they were one in the same, but this cannot be further from the truth. These two powerful energies are at opposite ends of the rainbow.

The word emotion comes from the Latin verb *motere,* which means to move or to excite. Emotions make you move; they make you act in an excited manner. We see this all time when we watch sports. We see football players jumping up and down after making one play even though the game is far from over. But, just because we see players jumping all over the field and looking like they are into the game, does this mean that emotions are good? Do the Gods encourage the show of emotions?

Some would say the expression of emotions on the field is vital to achieving victory. They would comment on how much emotion and fire the player or team played with. But a closer examination shows this emotive state is not as advantageous as one might think...

The excited and agitated state of emotion is in stark contrast to what the mystics seek. Whether it is the Zen Buddhist, the Christian Monk or the Native American Vision Quest, the seeker is looking to *still* his emotions and desires so he can *feel.* It is the quieting of emotions that is at the heart of every enlightened experience. Emotions, the mystic would say, are the root of all our personal suffering on this earth. Whereas feelings are at the core of reality and are the answers we need when we are suffering inside.

The word "feel" in the dictionary is defined by such words as intuition, awareness, compassion and perception. None of these words comes to mind when talking about or experiencing emotion. Emotions, like we see on the field, usually indicate some connection with the Major Gods of Ego, Fear or Low Self Esteem. Is the player who is pounding his chest and doing dances in a state of awareness and compassion or is he on an ego high?

Emotions and Feelings are not the same. When you see wild displays of emotion during a game it's a sign from the Gods that the player or players in question really aren't sure of their ability or of the outcome of the game. Just watch sometime and you'll see what I mean. It's always the team with the players that are focused and quiet that end up winning the game. That's because they are *confi-*

dent. They don't have to run around screaming it. It just oozes out of them natu-rally. You never saw Michael Jordan or Joe Montana thumping their chests. You never saw the 98' Yankees out of control even as they were winning 125 games and the World Series. It was as if they were in a meditative state, focused and quiet. Philosopher and author Robert Pirsig summed it up perfectly in an obser-vation he made in his novel *Lila* when he wrote about religious fanaticism. He said, and I'm paraphrasing, that you never see people running around screaming when they see the sun come up everyday because they *know* the sun is going to come up everyday. There's no need to pronounce the obvious.

In sports or in life, the confident athletes play in silent self-assurance. The ones who lack confidence have to use emotions to try and convince themselves that they are good. But emotions are by their nature flighty, unpredictable and with-out depth, whereas feelings are rooted in the soul and are eternal.

Off Season...

After the long season has come to an end, we clean out our lockers and head into the off-season. The days shorten, the wind blows colder and our thoughts move away from the field of battle and into the nebulous world of self-reflection on the season passed. It is an important time, maybe the most important time of all, because this is the time when we can gather up our experiences, sit with them and *learn.*

As we play our games during the season, it is sometimes hard to pull back and reflect. There are always too many distractions that come from worrying about our results. But in the off season there is a large void of time that brings with it the opportunity for silence and solitude, which is the perfect setting for soul to understand and grow. And that leads me to my last question...

NOW THAT I KNOW WHAT MY PROBLEMS ARE HOW CAN I FIX THEM?

If I had to think of one thing that most everyone has in common it is the resistance to *change*. I don't care who you are the thought of changing something about yourself, which you have been living with your whole life, is frightening. Change has always been synonymous with death and death is not something any of us want to face. But what we need to realize is that change will come anyway whether we want it to or not and we can be dragged to it kicking and screaming or we can face it and move on. Change is what the Gods are all about. You're better off surrendering to it now because if you don't then your life will become one endless struggle against an invincible opponent.

There are varying degrees to the amount of change you may need to make, but one thing must be clear. If a God is showing you something about yourself then you *must* transform that something into something *different*. It may be extreme, as in the case of the yips, or less dramatic like learning to deal with the fear of hitting with two strikes, but ultimately, you *must* become a different person and you must change your energy if the Gods are to be appeased and the lesson is to be learned. Otherwise you will never *grow*.

What many people will say when faced with change is that "things could always be worse" or "I've been successful so far so why should I change?" But what they're missing is the fact that the Gods don't care if you are a "success" or that "things could be worse". Material success is at the bottom of the list with the Gods and things could *always* be worse. They just want you to *learn*. Sure, you can be a three hundred hitter in the Major Leagues and be afraid of hitting with two strikes on you; but that isn't the point. The point is that you have a fear inside you that needs to be faced and *must* be faced because it will haunt you on and off the field for the rest of your life if you don't. Remember, the Baseball Gods aren't just interested in your life on the baseball field they are interested in your *life*.

The point I've been trying to get across here is that the Gods want you and everyone else on this planet to have more awareness, not just a three hundred batting average or a spot in the Hall of Fame. There are plenty of unhappy people who are in the Baseball Hall of Fame. What I'm talking about is the Hall of Fame of the Spirit and that is a much loftier aspiration...

There are many times in our lives when we run into people we haven't seen for a while and we are struck by how different they appear. They act differently, talk differently, give off a different *energy* and sometimes even *look different*. When we ask them what happened and why they look so different, they usually recount a long journey into themselves where they just simply changed their entire lives. These people had faced some kind of trauma and had emerged from it, not broken, but better for it. They looked at every aspect of their lives and then made the changes. The Gods are good that way. They will pin point it for you so you don't have to guess, but then it's up to you to make the changes.

With most of us a "total overhaul" is not needed. Most of the time it is one or two sticking points that need to be faced while the rest of us remains in tact. But still, the effect of facing even one fear can appear like it is a total life changing experience because this is a serious business folks; these are *Gods* we are dealing with. And when you face a fear in your life you will find that it will reverberate all the way down to the core of your being. It will shake your foundation and it *will be* a death like experience. All change is a death like experience. But, as with all death, there is a promise of rebirth waiting on the other side...

What needs to be done with issues is to confront them head on. This may sound simple and obvious, but most good solutions are often simple. If you are petrified of hitting with two strikes then *make* yourself hit with two strikes. If you are afraid of throwing a three and two curveball with the bases loaded then *throw* a three and two curve ball with the bases loaded. If you are an Ego driven ball player who doesn't care about anyone but his own needs, then put your own needs aside for once and give unconditionally to the team. If you have control problems because you have no control over your life or are being controlled by someone else, then do what it takes to *take* control of your life. If you are someone who is afraid to be alone then *be* alone. If you are selfish, *give.* If you are afraid to stand up for yourself then *stand up* for yourself. If you are repressed then *express* yourself. If you always wanted to be a pilot, or a carpenter or own a business then just go do it. Because, when you do, something will happen. You will *feel* different and these feelings will be the thing that will guide you to your true self. It may not be pretty at first and you may make some blunders initially, but your *willingness* to face the issues and the *personal accountability* it requires to do so will guide you through the rough spots. And things *will* work out in the end. They always do for people who endeavor to become more aware. Remember, the goal is never "did I win?" or "am I successful?" but instead "did I *learn?*"

Change is tough. I understand this. But it is essential to growth. If the caterpillar isn't afraid to change into a butterfly then why should you be afraid? You will survive and you will be better for it. Now, I know I'm making it sound so simple and easy, but, like I said earlier, the best answers to problems are not in the gray area of complexity, but in the clear light of simplicity. It's just hard for us to face the simple truths because they're so direct and to the point and they require us to *change!* When we complicate things we *delay* the change we need to make.

Change also means that your life is never going to be the same. And that scares you. But you must remember that's what you're here for! When things stop growing they begin dying. Your life isn't going to get *worse* because of the healthy changes and growth you make. It means your life is going to get *better*. Like everything else it's just a matter of perspective. Remember change, which is synonymous with evolution, always makes things better. That's what evolution does; it keeps adjusting and improving on the present situation. It's only when we *fight* change and evolution that things get worse and become *extinct*.

Last thoughts on Energy

Throughout this book I've been making my case for energy as reality. I have done this by introducing you to the Baseball Gods who are the keepers and manipulators of this energy in the baseball world. It is hard for people to see energy as the prime reality because it is invisible and not tangible like the physical world we experience with our five senses. But, what I hope I have shown here is that, although energy is invisible, it does *become* the tangible everyday material reality we see...

There are two wells from which I have drawn when searching for proof that energy is the prime reality. The first was Western Science and the Second was the Art of Eastern Meditation. The two are separated by the obvious philosophical differences between east and west. The west is science/substance based and the east is spiritually based, but they are, in reality, *exactly* the same. They are opposite sides of the same coin.

In Western Science, what Quantum Physicists have found, as they've gone deeper and deeper into the atom, is that the source of all material things is invisible energy! What this means is that if you went deep inside the cells that make up a bat, for instance, you would eventually get to the point where it becomes nothing but pure energy. There would be no substance left. It would only be invisible energy. And what this means is that the bat you see and hold in your hand is not really there! It is an illusion. It's only there in the form of a bat because of the way nature manipulates energy and the way we manipulate nature. Nature turns the energy into the components that make up the bat, wood, and we turn that wood into a bat! But it is at its source pure energy...

Mediation, like Quantum Physics, also looks at the material world as illusionary, but it comes to that conclusion from a different perspective. It focuses on the invisible world of feelings as opposed to the invisible world of energy as the prime reality.

There are many different methods of meditation, from one point, to focused breathing, to mantras, to Zen, but the effect is still the same. It separates us from the physical/mental reality we live in and delivers us to a higher level of consciousness. It all sounds otherworldly, but it is something we have all experienced at one time or another. I talked about these *feelings* earlier when I covered the God of Love. If you have ever loved something more than yourself then you have connected with the universal energy that binds us all and creates us all. It is something that cannot be described in words. It has to be *felt*.

But meditation, though esoteric to westerners, has made some inroads into our scientific culture. It is a fact that meditation lowers a person's blood pressure and heart rate. It is a fact that there are masters who, in a meditative state, can hold their hand over a flame and *not be burned*, while others can drop their heart rate to just a few beats per minute. They have learned that the physical reality is only an illusion that can be manipulated into whatever they want it to be.

There are scores of examples where masters of meditation can achieve super human results, even the power to heal the fatally ill. I was reading a book once about a Native American Medicine man called Rolling Thunder who in his meditative state was able to literally *pull* the diseased energy (cancer) out of a person and into himself where he then assimilated it and vomited it out of his system. It is an event that has been documented as valid by medical doctors and is a perfect example of how, when one is connected with the energy that makes up life, one can manipulate it and change it! This is not theory I'm talking about; this is factual and empirically verifiable. It may not fit into what we understand in our culture, but that doesn't mean it doesn't have validity.

Today's western physicians, with their biological based medicines, have done wonderful things manipulating energy on a physical level and in many cases this has been enough to counteract the destructive energy in the sick person's body, but it is limited and archaic compared to the pure energy of the spirit.

When I was in college, I took a nutrition class and the professor told a story of a fatally ill cancer patient who was given a few months to live. Medical Doctors had given up all hope and had taken him off all medications. He was told he was going to die and that he had best prepare for the end. But this man, despite his fate as determined by doctors, came to the conclusion that he was not ready to die and that what was missing from his life was laughter and joy. So, he bought every tape he could find of his favorite movies and television comedies and he began to watch them all day and night. He laughed and laughed and felt the flood of positive energy fill his body. Three months later his cancer was in complete remission and three months after that it was gone!

Now, when one looks at this story the key words that pop out are laughter and joy, not pills and drugs. He cured himself not with a biological solution, but with something that has no material connection to the world at all. His *laughter* and *joy* couldn't be weighed or measured; they had to be felt. They were not *made of anything*; they were pure positive energy, which, when tapped into, had the power to change his physical reality. *That's the point I'm trying to make about the Gods.* They can't be measured empirically; they exist outside of our literal translation of life. They exist in the love we feel...

Life is a mysterious event. Science says the energy we are made of is neither created nor destroyed. The bodies we have and the energy that they are made of will someday change form, but will never disappear. So the question must be asked: "Does this immortal energy exist in the forms we see because it's trying to tell us something or is it just a freak chemical reaction? Is it possible that the life we live is one of many grades in a school we hope to one day graduate from?" At this point, I don't know the answers to those questions, but I do know that to call the transient objects of the material world "reality" is to miss reality. And if one examines the history of western culture one can conclude that it certainly hasn't gotten us anywhere so far. Sure we may have computers and microwave ovens, but in case you didn't know it, in the decade of the nineties, 100 million people died because of wars fought over the belief in the material reality...

Last thoughts on Mechanics and the Material Reality

Throughout this book I have been tough on the material reality. I've given it a pretty short rift, but I think that's because it is so central in people's reality that it needed to be knocked down a peg or ten. But now that I've cleared it out of the way it makes it easier to look back at it with a more forgiving tone.

Having the correct mechanics in baseball are essential to playing the game at a high level. If you are a pitcher you have to get on top of the ball or you won't throw effective strikes. If you're a hitter you have to keep your hands and weight back during the swing or you won't hit the ball well. But where the mistakes come in is when we think these mechanics come *before* everything else. And that is just not the case. (The only time where mechanics do come to the fore is when an injury occurs and forces one to change ones mechanics or when the body tires and changes the mechanics on its own. But, in each case, it still comes down the player's ability to understand what the Gods are trying to tell him. If a player is injured then the Gods want him to understand what the energy of the injury is trying to tell him. And in the case of being tired because of fatigue or age the player needs to be flexible enough to realize that he is tired or too old to compete the way he used to in his youth and change, which means he must let go of his Ego!)

Every player and every physical body of every player has the capacity to have good mechanics all on it's own. The body and mind knows what it has to do in order to perform naturally. It can figure that out with its own intelligence. But it is the spirit of the individual that's trying to evolve, which gets in the way of the body and mind as they try to perform in the real world of baseball. And it is these struggles that give the individual *insight* into the lessons he needs to learn in life.

Hot Stove League

After the season is over and the action on the field has faded, the Hot Stove League begins to heat up. The Hot Stove League was named in the early 20th Century for those late fall and winter nights when Owners, General Managers, Coaches and Fans would gather around the Hot Stove to examine what went right and what went wrong over the past season. They'd address the problems and then propose solutions. They'd ask questions and they'd search for answers.

I have asked many questions throughout this book and I've tried to put forth answers. I hope the answers I've found will be of use to you in your own search. There are an infinite number of paths to heaven and all that matters is that you're on one of them…

I consider myself the luckiest man in the world...

When Lou Gehrig spoke these famous words in his farewell speech at Yankee Stadium, as he was dying of a disease that would later carry his name, he was expressing his love for the game of baseball. It was a pure love that has been felt by all, understood by few and forgotten by far too many. It was a love that guided him through the shadow of death and into immortality....

What I have found over the past forty years of playing the game of baseball is a feeling of pure love. And isn't that what you think of when you think of a God, or a Creator? I do. I believe, from the beginning of time, god has only been one thing and that one thing is pure and innocent love. The kind of love a young boy feels when he puts on his uniform and runs out on to the field for the first time and waves to his mother and father. Or maybe the kind of love a forty two year old man feels when he wakes up on a Sunday morning and knows he has two games to play. And though the games may be played in front of not one single fan, he doesn't care; the air is warm, the grass is green and the glove in his hand feels like an old friend. And, for a little while at least, he is a boy again. And it's opening day...

Extra Innings

I started writing this book in the spring of 2004 and in it I have chronicled everything from my earliest days as a Little Leaguer right up through the 2004 Men's Senior Baseball League season, which I have been a part of for the last eight years. In total I have spent the better part of the last forty years playing, coaching or watching the game of baseball.

Now, it is the fall of 2005 and I'm finishing up the last of what has become a bushel full of re-writes and edits. And during this editing process another baseball season has come and gone carrying with it a bevy of new lessons, as well some timeless classics. The road keeps winding ever higher with a surprise around every bend just as it was meant to be.

Of the challenges I've faced this season, many were familiar like the Gods of Fear and Self Esteem, but there was a also a new energy that seemed to be popping up everywhere I turned. It was the energy of *trying too hard* and it surfaced on my Men's League Team as well as with my favorite Major League Team, the New York Yankees. Because, you see, it doesn't matter if you're an aging geezer like me playing in a men's amateur league or a Major League Baseball Player, the Gods do not discriminate; they knock on everyone's door...

I'm sure you heard something about the Yankees dysfunctional season. It was so well chronicled in the media that no one could escape it. Here in Yankees country all we heard about day after day and week after week was how the team was *pressing*, couldn't *relax* and was *trying too hard*.

As with every energy issue that a ball player or team confronts, the Major Gods of Ego, Low Self Esteem and Fear are usually somewhere in there mixing it up. All issues are birthed from these powerful gods and it's pretty tough to relax when one is under their spell. Our natural reaction is to keep trying harder and harder to *overcome* these Gods, but it's a fool's game that ultimately keeps snowballing until the player or players become frozen and incapable of performing at their full capacity. If you watched the playoffs this year you saw evidence of it nearly every night.

The question is how do we stop ourselves from trying to hard when we want something so badly? The answer to the question points immediately to issues of

Self Esteem and Fear. We need to figure out why it is so important for us to achieve whatever it is that we're trying to achieve and what we're so afraid of if we don't.

A player who tries too hard isn't one with the game; he is outside the game trying to dominate *it* like an invading virus. But no one person is bigger than the game and that is what he must learn. If a player comes up in a big spot where he *wants* to hit a homerun so he could be a *hero,* he is no longer a blank slate who reacts to the situation and is one with it; instead, he is easy prey for the Gods. He will no longer be in balance and in the moment. He will be just ahead of or behind the moment and will just miss the pitches he should hit hard and will swing at the pitches he shouldn't. We see it happen all the time. It is a sure sign that the player is falling victim to the Gods and they are making a mess of the situation.

So what can a player do? How can he relax and not try too hard?

The player who is in the middle of any crisis must first be able to step back and admit that he is having issues. This, of course, is not an easy thing for anyone to do on his own, but it is something a coach can initiate by pointing out the *facts,* which the player is too *blinded* to see. These facts will vary from player to player, but they most certainly will stem from any one of the Major or Minor Gods. It is the coach's job to zero in on what God is torturing the player, what issue or issues he is having and then to start that player down the road to self-awareness. The best coaches are part therapist, father figure or mentor. These qualities are equally as important as having a superior knowledge of the game.

A coach becomes vital in these situations and his importance to the team becomes elevated above the guys who are actually playing the game. I talked about some of things a coach can do to help a player with energy issues earlier in the book, but those were long-term solutions. In the case of a player who is trying too hard in short series, like some of the stars we saw in this year's playoffs, the tactics are different. A short-term emergency approach is needed.

What a coach must do at this point is to *simplify* things for his player, which in turn helps the player to get out of the grasps of whichever god is hounding him. He must help his player to become a blank slate again and he can do this by tapping into the earliest fundamentals of the game, which will hopefully return the player temporarily to the childlike state of innocence he once had when he learned the game for the first time. This will clear out the muddled picture, at least for a while. Of course, all of this is dependent on the player's willingness to *let go* of his ego and to *trust* the coach.

What the coach must help the player to see and to feel is the need to just concentrate on the ball. The player has to participate in a type of one point meditation where he steps up to the plate and thinks of *nothing else* but seeing the ball all the way until he hits it. That's it. He can forget about trying to pull the ball or hit it up the middle or to the right side and he can certainly forget about the mechanics of hitting. None of that will work because he first needs to *see the ball* in a clear and unfettered state.

Now, I know what you're saying. You're saying: "*are you kidding me?*" There has to be more to it than that! But, if you really stop and think about it, you'll see that the whole problem is the player's inability to see the ball clearly because he is so blinded by either staring into the sun of his own ego, cowering in the face of his darkest fears or falling victim to his low self worth. All these energy issues blind him and block his ability to see the ball.

A way to understand this further is by looking at a player who is performing at the top of his game. Have you ever heard a player being interviewed when he is hitting the ball well? If you have then you will always hear him say something to the effect that he is *seeing the ball* well or *picking the ball up right out of the pitcher's hand*. Remember, it's usually the simple answers that work. See the ball; hit the ball. That's it…

The body, which includes the mind, is an amazing instrument. If you stop and think about everything it does on a daily basis just to keep us alive it is staggering. And what's even more staggering is that we, meaning our conscious state, have very little if anything to do with it! We don't tell our lungs to breath and to absorb oxygen in the alveoli and then to release carbon dioxide out through our breath, but they do it on a constant basis every second of the day. In fact, one can say that most of what the body does it does independent of our "consciousness" and with the utmost perfection. It has, in a way, a life of its own. And with that in mind, don't you think our bodies have the capability to do what it takes to hit the ball anytime it wants? Of course it can if we let it. But the Gods impede our miraculous body every step of the way. And they're supposed to until we can achieve the same level of awareness with our spiritual energy that our body does with its physical energy. That's the whole point of life, to marry the physical world of substance with the spiritual world of feelings, together as one and bound by the *energy* of life…

As I come down to my final few thoughts, I keep coming back to the same image that I've been describing throughout this book and that is the image of energy binding all things together, from the smallest particles in our cells to the deep and timeless love we feel for this beautiful game...Life is indeed meaningful and the proof is everywhere around us...

It's late October now and the weather outside my New England home reeks of Indian Summer. I think I'll grab my glove and my ball bag and go outside to throw a few balls up against the mattress...

978-0-595-39732-7
0-595-39732-8

Printed in the United States
53961LVS00005B/340-357

9 780595 397327